Look Up!

I0833767

Look Up!

Solve What Matters

Kimberly Andrikaitis

Look Up! Solve What Matters

Cover design by Janis Elko

Interior design by Exeter Premedia Services Private Ltd., Chennai, India

First published in 2026 by
Business Expert Press, LLC
222 East 46th Street, New York, NY 10017
www.businessexpertpress.com

ISBN-13: 978-1-60649-566-7 (paperback)
ISBN-13: 978-1-60649-567-4 (e-book)

Portfolio and Project Management Collection

First edition: 2026

10 9 8 7 6 5 4 3 2 1

EU SAFETY REPRESENTATIVE
Mare Nostrum Group B.V.
Doelen 72
4831 GR Breda
The Netherlands
gpsr@mare-nostrum.co.uk

To Dad, who taught me that sticking your head in the ground will result in getting your ass kicked—and to Mom, who always helped me get back up.

Description

Scrum Masters, Project Managers, Agile Coaches, and Delivery Leaders: You're probably tired of being questioned, undervalued, dismissed. You know you're making a difference, but you're *struggling to prove it to the people signing your paycheck*. Layoff rumors aren't just whispers anymore—you're watching friends and colleagues lose their jobs while facing an increasingly brutal job market.

And despite all this turmoil, one thing remains unchanged: You are an experienced professional who knows your stuff.

The complaints your leaders grumble about—"Agile was supposed to fix this mess" or "Everyone looks busy, but nothing is getting done"—aren't isolated. They're persistent grievances pointing to the same underlying issue: ***sweeping dysfunction that no amount of team improvement can fix.***

So, what's happening?

Let me be blunt: **You've been solving the wrong problems**. See, if most of your energy goes into team-level work while organizational chaos above undermines everything you do, you'll keep banging your head against the same four walls. Over and over again. This is both exhausting and bad for your head.

But here's the silver lining: beneath each frustration lies an **opportunity in disguise**. *The delivery professionals who become truly indispensable*—the ones who get promoted, funded, and trusted with exciting challenges—*are the ones who **solve system issues**, not just team issues.*

Are you ready to join them? This book shows you how.

Contents

Endorsements

"An overused Agile coaching adage is, 'ask the team.' I've said it myself countless times. Sometimes, though, the root cause of a problem is beyond the team. In those cases, Kimberly Andrikaitis encourages us to 'look up.' That means looking above where the symptom appears. Looking up may uncover issues in strategy, goals, leadership, the system, and more."—**Mike Cohn, Author of *User Stories Applied, Agile Estimating and Planning,* and *Succeeding with Agile***

"Having developed thousands of people in the skills, discipline, and beingness of Agile coaching, I often tell them, 'There are roses scattered at your feet.' By this I mean that the team level is where the action happens—and where vital information for the rest of the business is born—yet too often it's uncollected, misunderstood, or lost in translation. Look Up! Solve What Matters. *connects the dots, showing practical, no-nonsense ways to turn those "roses" into usable insights that lead to better business decisions. What I love most is that Kimberly wraps this guidance in relatable stories and a straightforward, super-usable style that makes you want to put it into action right away."* —**Lyssa Adkins, leadership coach/consultant and author of *Coaching Agile Teams***

"Kimberly has pulled off something impressive. She is able to perfectly describe the situation that delivery change agents find themselves in, without getting stuck proposing another band-aid for another well-worn team challenge. Instead, she uses her hard-earned experience to encourage delivery professionals to look up, out, and beyond … to find the true source of the challenges teams face. This book will be an eye-opener for many delivery change agents who are frustrated that the conventional advice they've been following doesn't work. This book shows a different path forward."—**David Frink, executive coach, Frink Consulting**

"Look Up! *is a breath of fresh air in the delivery space. With its informal tone and creative examples, it feels more like a conversation with a trusted friend than a lecture from a self-proclaimed guru.*

Kim's perspective on delivery professionals as delivery change agents is especially powerful—it highlights the real value these roles bring to teams and organizations. Kim doesn't just focus on making teams better. She shows you how to look up and see the organizational dysfunction that's creating the problems everyone's trying to solve.

Each chapter walks readers through familiar challenges (from demonstrating your impact to leadership, to spotting the systemic issues that crush team productivity) and offers practical, grounded approaches for addressing them. The 'Connect the Dots and Take Action' chapters are excellent, giving you specific tools to influence both your team and the broader organization.

This book is a must-read for delivery professionals looking to level up from good to great. Whether you're a Scrum Master, Project Manager, or Agile Coach, it's an essential guide for anyone ready to expand their impact beyond just facilitating meetings. Kim teaches you to become the strategic partner leaders actually need.

Relatable, insightful, practical—and fun. Enjoy the journey."—**Tom Wessel, Lean-Agile Consultant and Trainer, Cofounder of TriAgile**

"Kim really nails it with her latest offering, Look Up! Solve What Matters. *Finally, addressing a real gap in how we think about Agile. Leaders often feel pushed to the sidelines when they should be genuinely involved. This book provides tangible methods and guidance on how leadership and Agile can effectively work together. If, as a leader, you've felt caught between staying engaged and respecting your team's autonomy, it's a must-read."*—**Jim Grundner, Founder and CEO, TekAdvizr**

"Teamwork matters, but this book highlights lasting change when we also look up to the system that's shaping the teams."—**Tricia Broderick, Coauthor of *Lead Without Blame*, Founder of Ignite Insight + Innovation**

Acronym List

AI—Artificial Intelligence

API—Application Programming Interface

CEO—Chief Executive Officer

CIO—Chief Information Officer

CTO—Chief Technology Officer

DOWNTIME—Defects, Overproduction, Waiting, Non-utilized talent, Transportation, Inventory, Motion, Excess processing

EQ—Emotional Intelligence

IT—Information Technology

NPS—Net Promoter Score

PDF—Portable Document Format

PO—Product Owner

PTO—Personal Time Off

QA—Quality Assurance

RCA—Root Cause Analysis

ROI—Return on Investment

SPOF—Single Point of Failure

WIP—Work in Progress

Foreword

It's mid-2025 and we've hit a perfect storm in the agile space. Practitioners such as agile coaches and scrum masters are being laid off because stakeholders don't see their value. Artificial intelligence (AI) is disrupting the IT, Technology, and DevOps spaces, so again, agilists and other technology roles are being challenged. The world's economy is struggling, so that's a huge contributor. And our stakeholders are reviewing the impact their incredible investments in agile have returned and they're coming up nearly empty.

All these factors have struck at the golden age of agile transformations and disrupted people, jobs, and value propositions.

So, we've got to ask ourselves, what happened?

I'd argue, there are many contributors. But one of the most significant is the fact that we (agile consultants, coaches, scrum masters, change agents, RTEs, and experienced practitioners) what Kim has framed as delivery change agents, have made one fatal mistake. We looked down too much. We considered agile adoption to be a team-driven activity instead of a more holistic one.

That's why Kim's book is so timely and important. It comes at a time when agile practitioners need to look up and around at their agile contexts and begin to take a more systemic view to the requisite landscape for effective and powerful organizational change. Realizing that it's no longer a downward or a team thing. Realizing, in fact, that it never was.

The book begins its journey by setting the stage. I particularly like Kim's no-nonsense approach in her writing. For example, her assumption about the reader's capability is captured by this simple statement—*You, my dear reader, are an experienced professional who knows your shit.*

And she continues to be that clear and focused throughout.

After setting the problem scape in "The Awakening—The Question That Changed Everything" chapter, I was heartened to see Kim address what might be the hardest challenge for our community—proving our worth.

In "Investment Regret—Agile Was Supposed to Fix This Mess, Not Make It Worse," she gives us the tools to build real relationships with stakeholders and connect our work to what leaders care about. Not the fluff, but the business outcomes that matter. It's about being the strategic partner they can't ignore, which is exactly what we need right now.

"Customer Crisis—We've Gone From Delight to Damage Control" puts the customer first. Kim shows us how to become the dumpster fire spotter—identifying customer disasters before they happen and turning boring team updates into customer impact stories. It's shifting from damage control to customer delight. And making sure that leadership sees how our work *prevents* the crises that keep them up at night.

"Status Confusion—Everyone Is Busy, but Nothing Is Getting Done!" addresses the translation gap I see everywhere. This is where teams are doing great work, but leadership has no clue what's happening. Here, Kim digs into why stakeholders stop showing up to our demos and how technical jargon is making us invisible. She shows us how to make our work evident in ways that truly matter to the business.

"Resource Waste—We Are Bleeding Money at an Alarming Rate" is all about waste elimination. But not the obvious stuff. Kim goes after the sneaky productivity killers that are bleeding organizations dry. The unplanned work that derails everything. The context switching that's making people crazy. The "everything is urgent" mentality that paralyzes teams. So many organizations get trapped chasing shiny objects and biting off way more than they can chew. As delivery change agents, we need to recognize these wasteful practices and eliminate them.

How apt is the title "Competitive Disadvantage—We're Getting Crushed by Start-Ups Half Our Size." This is where the rubber meets the road in the book. Kim gets into the weeds with the DOWNTIME waste framework—giving us a systematic way to identify what's slowing us down. She explores T-shaped teams, knowledge silos, and why Susie can't take vacation. It's about building teams that can work together instead of waiting around for specialists. While action permeates throughout the book's journey, it comes to a head here. In other words, leading to actions that lean toward looking up!

Finally, I was delighted to see Kim return to center a bit with her inside-out focus in "The Reawakening—Building Your Foundation for

Success." She explores our inner patterns—how to receive feedback without falling apart, what really drives our motives, staying curious instead of judgmental, keeping our cool during conflict, and choosing our battles wisely. These active reflections are the most critical part of our delivery change agent success because that success is truly an inside-out job.

I was honored when Kim asked me to write this foreword. I've known her for a long time, and I deeply respect her experience and perspective. I was then blown away when I read her book and realized how consequential it is to our current context and futures.

This is a defining moment in our agile journey as delivery change agents. And Kim's book arrives just-in-time to help guide us toward a new generation of success among the chaos of this perfect storm.

I encourage you to read it. Digest and internalize every bit of it.

—Bob "Agile Moose" Galen
June 2025, Cary, NC

Acknowledgments

Writing this book has been a journey I couldn't have taken alone, and I'm grateful to so many people who made it possible.

To David Frink, who provided invaluable feedback on my very early drafts and whose coaching and leadership transformed my perspective—thank you for being the first eyes on this work and for your incredible mentorship. Your belief in my message made this slightly less terrifying.

To my incredible seed readers: Amy Batchelor, Betsy Atkins, Dan Parsons, Efrat Ware, Greg Smith, Jim Grundner, Katherine Howland, Lee Eason, Mary Stahly, Michael Huynh, Nancy Failla, Ryan Ragsdale, Scott McLellan, Steven Terry, and Tom Wessel—thank you for taking the time to read early drafts and provide thoughtful feedback that made this book so much better.

Bob Galen, thank you for writing the foreword and for being my teacher, confidant, and trusted adviser through and through. I'm beyond fortunate to be mentored by the one and only badass moose.

Mike Cohn, a genuine agile superstar—this fan girl is over the moon to receive your endorsement, marketing tips, and overall support in this endeavor. Thank you for everything!

Lyssa Adkins, I've been a huge admirer of your work for most of my career, from Coaching Agile Teams to the ICP-ACC course. Receiving your endorsement feels like validation from one of my professional heroes. Thank you for your generosity and for paving the way for all of us.

Kam Jugdev, for greenlighting this project and providing unwavering encouragement, support, and love.

To all my mentors, teachers, and support systems who have shaped my thinking, challenged my beliefs, and turned my frowns upside down:

Stephen Kellogg—My very first mentor; you showed that true leaders don't hurl office phones through walls.

David Moye—Who first introduced me to scrum, making me the agile dork that I am.

Cory Bryan—Thank you for taking a chance on this young foul-mouthed business analyst.

Mary Thorn—You exemplify unapologetic authenticity, paving the way for others. Never, ever change.

Maureen Green—For reminding me to trust my inner voice.

Mike Stocks—You inspired my entire coaching career.

Chris Risen—Sometimes we just need to put on our floaties.

Himanshu Shah—who taught me that the conflicts we have with others often reflect the conflicts we have within ourselves.

Patti Hellman—For teaching me to soften my stance and sweeten my words.

Rosemary James—Nope, the juice was rarely worth the squeeze.

Nelda Johnson—Those three words: "assume positive intent" changed everything.

Alessandro Dona—Thank you for teaching me a life-altering lesson of humility.

Srinivasan Manoharan—For your continued reminder to "flow like water, bend like bamboo."

Will Calhoun—For patiently explaining nerdy technological concepts in "Grandma" terms.

Ellen James—For continually putting things in perspective: "Life is too short for this hoo-ha."

Josh Bristow, Arien Williams—Your real-world stories and clear thinking shaped this book in meaningful ways.

Jim Grundner—We begrudgingly learned from one another and are both better because of it. I appreciate you.

Akeloe Facey—Who's never met a stranger. Thank you for reminding me to always walk in love.

To the amazing group of coaches I have had the opportunity to work directly with and learn from over the years: Art Pittman, Bruce Nix, Dan Parsons, Dana Pylayeva, Dick Bugg, Julee Everett, Leon Sabarsky, Paul Barrett, Peter Caradonna, and Tom Wessel. Each of you contributed lessons and opportunities that made me who I am today.

Janis Elko, beyond being an incredible graphic designer, you are the most effortlessly cool person I've ever known. Olive the Ostrich rocks!

Christine Hollinger, my bestie and constant support—is your mind blown?

To my family and friends, thank you for lifting me up and believing in me, especially Mom, who has always been my biggest cheerleader.

And finally, Eric: my husband, my rock, my person—Thank you for your patience, support, and loving strength throughout this process. You're the best. Xoxo.

Introduction

I wrote this book for the delivery professional who's tired of being questioned, who feels undervalued and misunderstood. *You* know you're making a difference, but you're struggling to prove it to the people signing your paycheck. You're passionate about delivery, dedicated to customers, and diligent about creating value—but somehow that's not translating into job security or recognition.

You're feeling unappreciated in your role, fighting daily resistance like an unwieldy boulder being dragged uphill. Layoff rumors aren't just rumors anymore—you're watching friends and colleagues get terminated while you face AI resume filters and mounting rejections in an increasingly brutal job market.

And despite all this chaos, one thing remains unchanged:

You are an experienced professional who knows your shit.

You *already* have the delivery fundamentals down—you know how to guide teams, improve processes, and deliver quality work. You champion continuous improvement, excel at productive conversations, and focus on delivering real value.

But those fundamentals? They're *just* the starting point. You can be the most skilled delivery professional in the world, but if you're only focused at the team level while the abovementioned organizational problems undermine *everything* you do, you'll keep banging your head against the same four walls. Over and over again.

How This Book Evolved

Two and a half years ago when I embarked on this book, my target audience was scrum masters specifically. As I developed the content, I began noticing the industry shift I describe later—and realized that my insights applied to *anyone* doing this essential work, regardless of their title.

From what I've observed, traditional agile roles have begun to fade—not because the work isn't valuable, but because organizations aren't seeing the return on investment (ROI) they expected. Meanwhile, the same essential responsibilities are now being distributed to people with different titles: project manager, delivery owner, enablement lead, and others who find themselves responsible for making teams work better together.

This gradual shift forced me to think differently about who really needs this guidance. Because it's not about the job title next to your name—*it's about what you actually do.*

If you're focused on helping teams deliver value faster, navigate organizational dysfunction, and create better outcomes for customers, then you're an "agile professional," or more specifically, a "delivery change agent."

A delivery change agent combines two essential qualities. First, you focus on delivery (bet you didn't see that coming!): getting quality software to customers on time and solving their real problems. It's not about frameworks or methodologies or magic spells; it's about results that make a difference.

Second, you have a flexible and curious mindset. You're not satisfied when people dismiss fresh ideas with a stale "but this is how we've always done it" corporate catchphrase. In fact, those eight words make you cringe. You ask smart questions, propose nifty solutions, and have the courage to experiment when something isn't working. You see problems others miss and you're determined to do something about them.

Whether you're labeled a scrum master, project manager, agile coach, delivery lead, or something else entirely, if the previous description fits what you do (or attempt to do), **this book is *for you*.** I don't want you thinking "that role isn't my role, so this book isn't for me." The title on your resume matters far less than the impact you make.

The Path Forward

The real challenge isn't proving your current worth—it's positioning yourself as someone who solves problems that organizations genuinely care about. I'm going to show you how to amplify your foundational expertise by teaching you to work more effectively on two levels: **team level** (by elevating your existing practices) and **systems level** (by recognizing and influencing the organizational patterns that either support or sabotage your efforts).

Most delivery change agents get trapped focusing only on what they can see and control directly (things such as team velocity, sprint commitments, or impediment removal). But when leaders are frustrated with delivery results, the problems they're complaining about usually point to something much bigger.

This book addresses five specific rants I hear repeatedly from leaders everywhere—complaints that consistently point to deeper organizational dysfunction. From "Agile was supposed to fix this mess" to "We're getting crushed by start-ups half our size,"—these aren't isolated problems. They're persistent grievances all pointing to the same underlying issue: system dysfunction that no amount of team improvement can fix.

But here's the silver lining: each of these rants is an opportunity in disguise. **When you can spot the system problems causing these complaints, you can become the person who illuminates them**. This approach will expand your influence *beyond* your team, position you as a strategic problem-solver, and drive the kind of organizational change that makes *you* invaluable as a trusted partner. In this book, you'll learn:

- How to identify the organizational patterns that create team struggles.
- Techniques for working strategically within dysfunctional systems.
- Methods for building deliberate relationships with stakeholders and leadership.
- Tools to strengthen your foundation so you can show up more effectively.
- Approaches for becoming the kind of delivery change agent others want to work with.
- And most importantly, how to position yourself as a critical partner (when the conditions allow for it).

This isn't *just* about making your team more efficient—it's about transforming how you show up *and* positioning yourself as someone who contributes to organizational improvement.

Your expertise, dedication, and emotional health are worth more than endless firefighting. This book will teach you to **look up** to uncover those systemic problems and opportunities others miss.

No Sugarcoating

Before we dive in, let's establish a few ground rules for our journey together:

- **This book won't cover every scenario.** The delivery world is vast and varied. I couldn't possibly address every unique situation you'll encounter, even if I wrote 1,000 pages (and trust me, neither of us wants that).
- **You'll need to apply critical thinking.** I'm providing principles, patterns, and practices—not a cookbook. You'll need to adapt these ideas to your specific context, stakeholder relationships, and organizational realities.
- **I'll be straightforward, even when it's uncomfortable.** I promise not to sugarcoat the challenges of being a delivery change agent. Sometimes the truth is messy, but that's where the real growth happens.
- **I assume you know the basics.** This book builds on foundational delivery knowledge. If you're new to concepts such as iterative delivery, continuous improvement, or stakeholder management, you might want to start with a more introductory resource.
- **Results aren't guaranteed.** What worked brilliantly in one organization might fail spectacularly in another. That's not a failure of the approach—it's the reality of complex human systems.

Think of these working agreements as our shared commitment. I'll provide honest and practical guidance drawn from real world experience, and you'll bring thoughtful application to your unique situation. Deal?

How This Book Is Structured

This book exposes five common leadership complaints that are turning your work life into a waking nightmare, along with bonus content on getting out of your own way. Each chapter digs into a specific dysfunction that's probably making you slightly crazy, but they connect—so read it straight through for maximum impact, or jump to whatever crisis you're facing right now.

We'll dive into these recognizable leadership grievances (along with what's really under the hood):

- "Agile was supposed to fix this mess, not make it worse" (*the delivery change agent's value challenge*).
- "We've gone from delight to damage control" (*customer satisfaction focus*).
- "Everyone is busy but nothing is getting done" (*visibility and communication issues*).
- "We are bleeding money at an alarming rate" (*hidden waste and productivity drains*).
- "We're getting crushed by start-ups half our size" (*efficiency and waste elimination*).
- (And your bonus!) Building your foundation for success (*personal development and self-mastery*).

Each chapter uncovers the hidden dysfunction driving these complaints and shows you how to become the go-to person for the problems *you* can solve.

Helpful Tip: If you're new to this "look up" approach, start from the beginning. If you're already thinking systemically but need help with a specific challenge, jump to what's most relevant and come back to fill in the gaps later.

Let's Do This

The delivery professionals who become truly indispensable are the ones who solve systemic problems, not just team problems. Look up! It's time to expand beyond the team and start influencing the organizational system.

CHAPTER 1

The Awakening—The Question That Changed Everything

Early in my scrum master career, I joined a global financial technology company that provided data, analytics, and workflow solutions across the capital raising process. With clients ranging from banks and public companies to institutional investors and wealth management firms, the stakes were high—any software defect could directly impact critical financial decisions and multimillion-dollar transactions.

Given the *literal mandate* to "make them deliver faster," I inherited a software development team that was struggling on multiple fronts. They were perceived as underperformers—slow to deliver, with production code plagued by defects and inconsistencies. The team was dispirited and disengaged, labeled as "underdogs" by the organization.

I, however, detected something very different. I envisioned what they *could* be: a powerhouse—a team with remarkable potential, skills, and drive to consistently achieve exceptional outcomes. They just needed some structure, support, and guidance.

But what I didn't see—what I *couldn't* see at that time—were the organizational forces working *against* them. I thought the problem was with the team because—well, *that's what I was told.* Looking back though, I can see that the team's struggles were symptoms of organizational dysfunction, not the problem itself.

During those first few sprints, I hung back, discovering the team's dynamics, building relationships, and documenting my observations (miscommunication, conflict avoidance, and distrust, just to name a few). I needed to understand the culture and challenges before potentially frightening them with a slew of off-putting changes.

Throughout the next few months, I helped the team adopt process improvements such as time boxing and story splitting. We refocused on the daily scrum event to center around that day's strategy, and not lifeless status updates. We held learning sessions to spread knowledge and insights among the developers. The team began to embrace quality as a collective concept and integrated unit testing into their development process. Rapport-building exercises, like show and tell, helped them establish unity, trust, and community from within.

I was doing everything I'd been taught to do—and doing it quite well, I may add.

Fast forward six months, they had been busting their butts, and the team was turning around. They had identified working agreements and began adhering to Definitions of Ready and Done. They were having heartfelt, honest conversations, and completing the work as predicted. The metrics showed a decrease in defects and velocity was on the upswing. I was proud of their collaboration, synergy, and increased delivery performance.

By every measure I knew how to track, they were winning.

This was around the time Lisa, the product manager, stopped me in the hallway. "Kim, quick question for you." I froze, feeling a sense of unwarranted dread. "I'm just wondering, as the team's scrum master, what ***do*** you ***do*** all day?"

I was completely taken aback and surprised to find myself mentally stumbling on the answer. *How could I respond to her question with a simple, well-articulated response, when I do so much? Wait a second. She's actually asking what I do? Is my value being questioned? Do I need to justify my position, my reason for existing here?* I mean, it sure felt that way. But I was also confused, because didn't the **company hire me** to **help this team succeed**? And by every measure I could see, we *were* succeeding. So, what exactly was I missing?

With a plastic smile plastered on my face, I responded. *Well, I facilitate scrum events, resolve impediments, and coach the team on the scrum framework.*

And even as the words left my mouth, I could feel how they *completely* missed the mark. She was quiet for a few beats before responding.

"Can't *anyone* do that?"

Ouch, that stung.

But it wasn't just the sting of criticism—it was something much deeper. Here I was, someone who had spent *months* transforming this team, guiding them through conflicts and celebrating their wins, witnessing their confidence grow, and their delivery improve. And to Lisa, I was just … replaceable. Interchangeable. Throwaway.

Can't anyone do that? The question hung in the air like a sharp slap to the face. She wasn't just questioning my performance, my experience, or my history—she was dismissing *everything I was* and everything I brought to the role. The hundreds of micro moments where I'd read the room perfectly, asked the hard question, or helped someone find their voice. In Lisa's mind, I was … insignificant.

But for now, let's set aside my wounded ego and focus on the obvious: Lisa didn't see the connection between the function of a scrum master and faster delivery—which is what she cared about.

And that's when it hit me—the measures I was tracking, such as team velocity trends and defect reduction, clearly weren't connecting to whatever Lisa was looking for. I was celebrating team wins while she was questioning why the organization needed scrum masters at all.

I mean, it was obvious that she wasn't connecting the dots between *my actions* and *her goals*. In retrospect, and I'm going to be perfectly honest here, I wasn't either. I was focused on team health; she was focused on business outcomes. We were having two completely different conversations.

Look, I knew to contain the daily scrum event to 15 minutes. I could recite the five scrum values in my sleep. I could explain (and perfectly spell) "empirical." I prided myself on my creativity: the numerous remote team building activities, the playful retrospectives, and the icebreaker questions. I was a textbook delivery change agent, perfectly executing everything I'd been trained to do. And that, my friends—was exactly the problem.

What I didn't realize then was that this awkward hallway interrogation wasn't unique to me, my skills, or even my company. It was happening to an entire category of delivery change agents—people whose job is to help teams work better together and deliver value faster.

Here's the thing: I don't care if you're called a scrum master, project manager, or chief happiness officer—if you're trying to help teams deliver better results, you are what I call a delivery change agent. And right now, delivery change agents everywhere are facing the same uncomfortable question: "What do you actually do?"

Many organizations are eliminating traditional agile roles without understanding that they still *desperately* need the value those roles can provide—just delivered differently. They *need* professionals who can speak the language of business outcomes, solve problems that span multiple teams, and contribute to executive-level decisions—they just don't realize it yet.

Years later, in another role at an entirely different company, I would face this **exact same** soul-crushing moment **again**. This time I was an agile coach (*a role I thought would give me more credibility*) and the questioner was Kevin, a program manager. The words were nearly identical: "As an agile coach, what do you actually do?" The sting was just as sharp, but the implications were even more troubling. If moving to a role with more leadership exposure didn't eliminate this line of questioning, what would?

That's when I started to see a pattern. It wasn't just Lisa or Kevin—I was struggling to connect with senior leadership *everywhere*. What I was doing, no matter how well I did it, did not resonate. And when budget cuts came, guess what? My role got eliminated (surprise!). Turns out, if you can't connect your work to problems leadership cares about, you become a target when times get tough.

But this time, I understood what was really happening—this wasn't about me, it wasn't about my skills, and it wasn't even about my specific role. **This was about an entire category of professionals whose primary focus was on teams, while significant dysfunction lived above us in the system.** We *were* solving real problems, but neglecting the bigger picture, like prescribing cough medicine while completely ignoring the lung infection.

What I didn't know then was that those two cringeworthy conversations were just early indicators of something much bigger brewing in our industry.

The Lisa Effect

What I experienced personally would soon become a widespread pattern that revealed something important: *organizations were eliminating roles without understanding the significant problems those roles could solve.*

While I struggled to articulate or demonstrate my value to leaders, entire organizations were beginning to question roles focused on delivery improvement, team coaching, and process repair. Sure, the work mattered—but was it worth paying specialists for? And even if it was, couldn't *anyone* perform it reasonably well?

The financial service industry saw particularly dramatic disruption, with major institutions such as Capital One, Lloyds Banking, Fidelity Investments, and others eliminating substantial numbers of scrum masters, agile coaches, and other delivery-minded professionals.

And … guess what? **While they cut these traditional roles, the underlying business problems didn't disappear.** Teams *still* struggled with predictability, quality issues continued to derail releases, and work visibility remained poor. The same challenges that originally drove organizations to shift to agility and hire scrum masters and agile coaches persisted. Shocking, I know.

What they didn't realize was that these were symptoms of deeper organizational dysfunction that no amount of team coaching could fix. They eliminated the people who were treating the symptoms, then wondered why the underlying problems got worse. The Band-Aid appliers were gone, but the wound kept bleeding—and now *no one* was trying to stop it.

Over time, many of these same organizations began posting new job openings—but with a twist. Instead of dedicated agile roles, they advertised traditional positions with agile responsibilities layered on top.

Take this "delivery program manager" position, for example. The core role is program management, but check out the additional expectations:

- "Ensure that scaled events take place and are productive and positive."
- "Facilitate prioritization and removal of impediments."
- "Ensure insight into process improvements to the organization."
- "Facilitate both strategic and tactical discussions."
- "Radiate information on progress to leadership and teams."

These layoffs and hiring patterns convey a very straightforward message: *Traditional agile roles are rapidly on the decline, but the underlying work remains essential.* It's just being distributed to people with different primary job functions.

And the opportunity here is massive because the path forward is clear: **delivery change agents must evolve from team-focused process facilitators to system-focused problem solvers who drive organizational success.** Those who make this shift will become the strategic partners organizations can't function without.

Look Up or Stay Invisible

Most delivery change agents operate at two different levels without realizing it—and the level they choose determines whether they'll become indispensable strategic partners or remain invisible contributors.

Looking at the Team

At the team level, we get trapped in what we can see and control directly: our team's velocity, the quality of our story refinement meetings, and the progress shown on the work board. We measure success by story points completed and impediments removed. This level is all about the team:

- "Our velocity increased by 15 percent this quarter."
- "We reduced our technical debt backlog."
- "On average, we're completing 87 percent of our sprint commitments."

Our conversations with the chief executive officer (CEO) sound like: *Our team is really clicking now. We're hitting our sprint goals and the retrospectives are generating good insights.* (And the CEO is thinking: So what? How does this help me?)

The problem isn't that looking at the team is wrong; teams absolutely need good practices. **The problem is that "only" focusing on the team leaves you invisible when budget cuts come.** You're solving symptoms while the real diseases remain untreated—and nobody with decision-making power can see your value.

Looking up at the System

At the system level the view is entirely different. Here we see organizational inconsistencies that strangle teams, competing priorities that dilute focus, and interpersonal politics that paralyze decision making.

This level is all about the system above us:

- "We eliminated a workflow bottleneck that was delaying every release by two weeks."
- "We identified why our metrics didn't connect to business value and worked with leadership to create measures that fundamentally matter to customers."

Here, our conversations with the CEO sound like: *We identified a system constraint that was costing us six weeks per release. We've implemented a solution that cut our deployment cycle in half while improving quality metrics.* (And the CEO is thinking: Oh yes, I like the sound of that!)

When you're obsessed with your team, and only your team, you remain invisible to leadership. When you look up at the system, you become indispensable.

Which delivery change agent would you eliminate first when budget cuts arrive?

It's Not Your Team, It's Your System

To understand what we're really fighting against, let's step into a familiar scene that plays out in organizations worldwide.

The View From the Top

Picture this. Three executives—the CEO, chief information officer (CIO), and chief technology officer (CTO) lean over their oval mahogany conference table, venting their frustrations. (No, this isn't the setup for a joke, although it might as well be.) Despite having talented teams and established processes, something fundamental isn't working.

The CEO leans forward, clearly frustrated. "Look, let's cut through the crap and just get to it. I don't understand why it takes so long to deliver a simple feature to our customers."

"I feel the same," the CIO replies. "In addition, our production incident tickets are through the roof! Why are our *customers* finding so many defects and not *us*?"

The CTO chimes in. "It's impossible to understand what is truly getting done. There is no view into the work."

"I cannot comprehend what we are paying these people for. What do they do all day?" The CEO leans back and closes her eyes. "Where is all of our money going?"

I've sat in way too many conversations like this and what happens next is laughably predictable: companies rush to "become agile." They often hire consultants who sprinkle agile pixie dust (usually in the form of daily scrums) and disappear, leaving behind teams that go through the motions while organizational dysfunction remains untouched.

But here's what those three very important executives couldn't see: yes, the problems they're describing have **symptoms** at the team level, but the *root causes lie in the system*. You can't solve misaligned incentives, unclear decisions, and competing priorities by improving team retrospectives.

The Four Blind Spots Crushing Your Teams

In my work, I've seen four systemic problems that consistently cause delivery chaos:

- Competing priorities *(decision-making dysfunction).*
- Knowledge bottlenecks *(workflow and capacity dysfunction).*
- Outputs over outcomes *(misplaced priorities).*
- Hidden waste *(process inefficiencies).*

But, before we dive deep into these four problems, let's make sure we're on the same page about what I mean by "systemic." I'm not talking about individual screw-ups or one-off team issues. Systemic problems are the ugly, messy organizational patterns that keep recreating the same headaches over and over again, no matter how many times you've "fixed" them.

Here's the difference:

- If your team keeps missing sprint commitments, that might be a team problem.
- If multiple teams keep missing commitments because leadership changes direction every other day, then it's probably a systemic issue—the problem lives in how your organization operates, not in the people doing the work.

Here's my completely unscientific but oddly accurate way to tell the difference. I call it the Head Banging Scale, and yes, it's exactly what it sounds like.

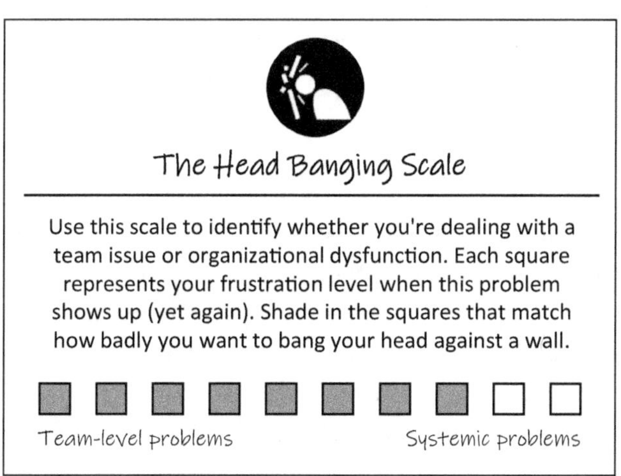

Here's how it works: On a scale of 1 to 10, how badly do you want to bang your head against the wall when this problem shows up again?

If you're shading just two or three squares, you're probably dealing with a team issue—something you can attack with better processes or clearer communication.

But if it's an 8, 9, or 10—if you're thinking: ARE YOU $^&* KIDDING ME, NOT THIS AGAIN!—congratulations, you've found a systemic problem. These are embedded in your company's DNA: the incentives, the culture, the unspoken rules, and the "way we've always done things." And I hate to break it to you, but you can't solve them by showing beautiful burndown charts or implementing new estimation techniques.

Problem One: Competing Priorities: When Everything Is "High Priority"

You've heard this conversation before:

What's the highest priority item?
They all are!
Yes, but which must be done first?
They all need to be done first!

When everything is the highest priority, nothing is. This exasperating situation wastes time in endless meetings rehashing the same conversations. Team morale plummets as people burn out trying to do everything at once. Truly important work gets delayed while everyone scrambles. And quality degrades when attention is divided and time runs out.

Problem Two: Knowledge Bottlenecks

I've seen this pattern repeatedly—the long-tenured developer who everyone depends on, or the specialized data team that becomes a major roadblock, or the legacy system only one person knows how to maintain.

Knowledge silos like this create delivery delays whenever key people are unavailable. They become single points of failure that can derail entire projects. Teams grow frustrated as work grinds to a halt waiting for one person or an external team. And creativity gets crushed when teams can't explore solutions without one person's blessing.

Problem Three: Outputs Over Outcomes—The "Busy but Nothing Gets Done" Syndrome

Every single leader I've worked with (and this is not an exaggeration) has shared the same staggering frustration: "The teams appear busy, but I don't know what's actually getting done." It's like they're watching shadows dance behind a curtain—they know there's movement, but they can't make out what's happening.

This (in)visibility problem stems from business value hiding behind garbled technical mumbo jumbo. Teams use approaches where nothing can be shown to customers until everything is finished. They focus on outputs (tasks completed) rather than outcomes (customer value delivered). And they rely on misaligned metrics that celebrate team efficiency while ignoring customer satisfaction. (*Seriously? If they aren't producing customer value, who cares if the team's predictability is 98 percent?)*

Problem Four: Hidden Waste—The Productivity Killers

While leaders naturally focus on visible costs like salaries and tools, some of the most expensive waste can be harder to spot (like baby weeds—harmless at first, but eventually they take over your entire garden).

The most expensive forms of waste? Unplanned work that derails commitments and destroys focus. Context switching that costs recovery time with every interruption. Excessive work in progress that creates the illusion of productivity while reducing actual output. And work that gets passed from person to person, or team to team, creating massive delays at each step.

These four problems might seem unrelated, but they all stem from the same root cause: **misaligned incentives that reward the wrong behaviors.** Which is exactly why team-level fixes often fail to stick—the organizational system keeps this dysfunction alive and well. Each of these wastes may appear minor in isolation, but combined they create death by a thousand paper cuts.

Your Moment to Act

After everything we've covered—the systemic problems, the blind spots, the pattern of role eliminations—you might be feeling a mix of validation and overwhelm. Validation because *finally* someone is naming what you've been experiencing. Overwhelm because this feels massive. Trust me, I know.

Let me be very clear: **This situation is *very* real. You are not imagining it and you're not alone.** Delivery change agents worldwide are facing these same challenges—the hallway interrogations, the budget cut rumors, and the struggle to demonstrate value. These aren't reflections of your skills or worth. They're systemic issues requiring systemic responses.

And although you can't single-handedly fix broken organizational structures or eliminate dysfunctional leadership patterns—you *can* shift your approach in ways that make your value undeniable and keep your sanity intact.

This means understanding what leaders ***really*** care about—not just what they *say* they care about, but what *truly* keeps them up at night. It means speaking the language of business outcomes instead of process improvements. Connecting your daily work to organizational goals that executives can see and measure. And building relationships with stakeholders who control resources and make decisions.

The journey starts where you are right now. You don't need to wait for the perfect organizational culture or ideal leadership support. You can begin making these adjustments immediately, in your current role, with your current team, in your current constraints.

The tools, strategies, and mindset shifts in this book will help you navigate whatever reality you're facing—whether that's supportive leadership or budget pressures, engaged teams or resistant colleagues, clear strategies or churning priorities.

Ready to begin? Let's start with the most fundamental challenge—making your impact visible when leadership questions whether agile fixed their problems or created new ones.

CHAPTER 2

Investment Regret—Agile Was Supposed to Fix This Mess, Not Make It Worse

Remember that cringeworthy hallway conversation with Lisa? The one where I couldn't adequately articulate my value as a scrum master? That humiliating moment revealed something crucial: *I'd been treating symptoms instead of the disease.* While I obsessed over team dynamics and candid conversations, I was blind to the broken systems above us *creating* these issues in the first place.

As a delivery change agent, you're in a unique position to spot what others miss. Leadership sees struggling teams and wants better execution (*which makes complete sense*). But *you* see teams being crushed by conflicting priorities, unclear authority, and organizational dysfunction. You're expected to improve team performance all while the underlying barriers live completely outside the team's control. How disorienting is that?

Remember how we discussed organizations blaming teams for systemic problems? That dysfunction is exactly what makes your value invisible: Companies hire agile consultants, implement frameworks *only* at the team level, and then declare victory ("Look! We're agile now!").

But are they? Sure, teams learned new techniques and processes—but everything above them *stayed exactly the same. These unfortunate teams are trying to be agile within a system designed for the exact opposite.* And you're caught in the middle, expected to *realistically fix things* while those barriers stay firmly in place.

This is where many delivery professionals get stuck. Scrum masters focus on team facilitation, project managers focus on schedules and budgets, agile coaches focus on practices—meanwhile, we're all missing the bigger opportunity to address the systemic problems that are truly holding the organization back.

And here's the hardest part: Your most important work—navigating the dysfunction, protecting your team from competing priorities, translating technical progress into business impact—is completely invisible to leadership. So, how can you demonstrate value when your best contributions leave no fingerprints?

Why No One Knows What You Do

This dynamic reminds me of professional theater productions. Some delivery change agents (such as scrum masters and agile coaches) are like the stage managers of a play. They're essential to the production's success, but unlike the actors who automatically generate applause, stage managers have to be more intentional about showcasing their impact. The ones who get recognized don't wait in the shadows—they find ways to make their contributions visible and get the recognition they deserve.

But not all delivery roles face this invisibility challenge. Project managers are more like the producers—they're visible, accountable, and leadership knows exactly who they are. They present status updates, they own budgets, and they get credit (*or blame*) when projects succeed or fail.

Even the most visible delivery roles struggle with this same fundamental challenge. When a play ends, the actors strut on stage for audience celebration and cheers. The director eventually emerges, bows, and accepts ample applause. The audience stands, whistling and whoo-hooing as these central figures bask in the lime light.

But what about the stage manager who coordinated every cue and the producer who made it all possible? Well, they have to be more strategic about getting their moment. The ones who *do* get their moment know how to position their work so their impact is undeniable.

Bringing this back to improving how teams deliver better, delivery professionals—whether they're the invisible facilitators or the visible coordinators—get overlooked when the product succeeds. The spotlight goes to the product itself and the developers who built it, not to the people who cleared the path and made the delivery possible.

Like air traffic controllers who guide thousands of flights or emergency dispatchers coordinating life-saving responses, delivery change agents often operate behind the scenes. **But the effective ones know how to make their impact visible and valued.**

So, how do you articulate and demonstrate your true value so that organizations understand the critical impact you bring to product delivery?

The Coffee Shop Revelation

Delivery change agents often struggle to demonstrate their true value in organizations completely obsessed with visible outputs. I learned this lesson during those uncomfortable hallway interchanges with Lisa and Kevin—conversations that still weigh on my mind today.

Setting aside the fact that my role was scrutinized (*twice!—yes, I'm counting*), there's a more obvious question: **Why *couldn't* I articulate my value, from an outcome-oriented perspective?**

I mean, I had no problem rattling off my *outputs* (removed impediments, facilitated scrum events, and coached the frameworks), but I couldn't express the why, the outcome of my actions. It was much like a stagehand listing "moved props" and "adjusted lights" without explaining how these actions created the magical atmosphere that transported the audience.

Then I learned about outputs versus outcomes. It happened in the most unexpected place—my neighborhood coffee shop.

It was a rainy Saturday, and I'd woken in a foul mood due to a poor night of sleep. I was lethargic. Groggy. Super cranky. Eric, my husband, and our two beloved dogs were intuitively keeping their distance, which further added to my annoyance.

I dressed and decided to walk to my neighborhood, locally owned café. The perky barista greeted me "Good morning! Vanilla cappuccino today? Grande?" (I go there often and rarely deviate from my preferred order). I nodded my head, paid for my coffee, and fell into the plushy patterned armchair to await my indulgence.

Several minutes later, a voice shouted out "Grande vanilla cappuccino for Kim!" I grabbed the steaming mug from the pickup counter and meandered back to my spot. The first sip was heavenly: Velvety, vanilla, creamy goodness. I closed my eyes, inhaled deeply, and slowly began to feel relaxation overtake me.

Sitting there, I watched as other customers collected their drinks. Some rushed out immediately, barely acknowledging their brew. Others stayed, but remained focused on their laptops, the coffee merely fuel for their work. Yet for me, this simple cup had transformed my entire morning—from stressed and irritable to centered and optimistic.

And then something important dawned on me. The barista's output was consistent: cups of coffee, prepared to order. But the outcomes varied dramatically for each customer. For some, it was just caffeine. For others, a habit. For me, it was transformative.

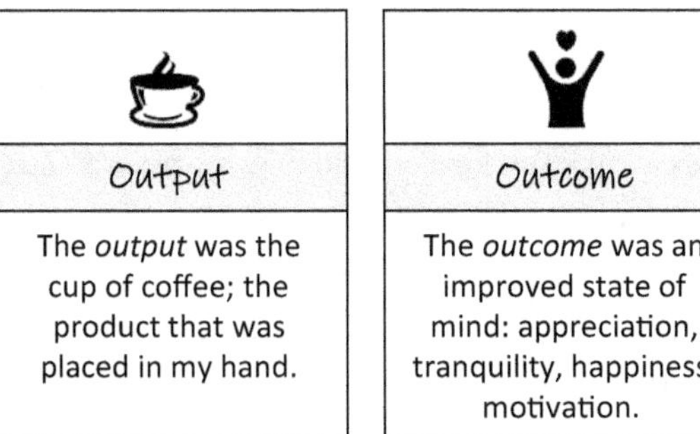

This mirrors our work as delivery change agents. While we can easily list our daily activities—our outputs—the *real value lies in the outcomes we create* for our stakeholders. Just as that cup of coffee had different meanings for different customers, our work impacts others in unique ways.

If you're sitting there thinking "Yeah, but I've been doing this delivery work for years and still can't explain my value."—I get it. I couldn't either, even after those hallway conversations with Lisa and Kevin. The coffee shop revelation didn't immediately fix everything. But it gave me a framework to start thinking differently. And that's all you need right now—just a different lens.

The Bridge Leadership Can't See

This same principle applies to your work as a delivery change agent. You create outputs—documented decisions, impediment logs, team agreements—that benefit the team but remain invisible to leadership. What they *do* see (or *should* see) are the outcomes: teams making faster decisions, quality improving, momentum maintained.

But here's the problem: you're probably talking about what you *do* (facilitate retrospectives, remove impediments) while leadership cares about the business results those activities create. This disconnect is even *harder* for delivery change agents because your contribution is often more difficult to measure than other roles. The actual things you create *do exist*, they're just not as immediately visible.

Think about it: developers produce code that creates valuable increments—*highly visible stuff.* Product owners (POs) create roadmaps, write stories, and build backlogs—again, everyone can see what they're doing. But delivery change agents? We create team agreements, metrics dashboards, and impediment logs. Useful? Yes, 100 percent. Obvious to leadership? Not so much.

Here's what we *primarily* create—the stuff that matters but nobody sees: We facilitate focused discussions that cut through the bullshit so teams can make informed decisions. We challenge people to solve their own problems instead of always running to us. We promote engineering practices that prevent disasters before they happen. We model transparency and trust so teams collaborate effectively instead of pointing fingers. We remove impediments so teams maintain momentum.

We know that these actions ultimately help the company achieve results, but it's like we reside in a secret society where **only** we know. And here's what's most maddening about this: *How do you demonstrate value when your best work leaves no fingerprints?*

This is where the rock star delivery change agents leave the others in the dust: **they deliberately connect (or bridge) their outputs to the outcomes leadership primarily cares about.**

Instead of proudly declaring "We had a great retrospective!" (*big yawn*), they connect directly to business impact: "Our kick ass retrospective helped the team spot and obliterate three major bottlenecks, slashing our delivery time by 40 percent and letting us respond to customer feedback twice as fast!"

Now, imagine if you brought systems-level outcome to the forefront of everyone's mind? Things like "I eliminated the chaos of seven competing priorities by driving leadership to ruthlessly prioritize their top three. The teams delivered 60 percent faster and customers quickly received the features they'd been begging for." Now you're not just improving team performance—you're solving the organizational dysfunction of strategic whiplash that naturally drives business results.

As you well know, this connection doesn't *magically happen* while you're sipping your soy milk vanilla latte. It takes intentional effort to track, measure, and shout from the rooftops how *your* actions directly contribute to the metrics that leadership obsesses over. Without building this bridge (from outputs to outcomes), your amazing work stays locked in that secret society, invisible to the very people who could champion your value.

Leaders Don't Care About Frameworks

First things first: you need to figure out what truly matters to your leaders. What drives their decisions? What keeps them awake at night?

After countless conversations with department heads, C-suite executives, and program managers, I've learned something you may find shocking:

Leaders don't care about scrum, kanban, or scaled agility, and so on. They care about business results.

And you already have the skills, mindset, and resourcefulness to help them achieve those results—you just need to connect what you do to what they want.

- How can you support leadership's goals?
- What questions should you be asking?
- What problems should you be investigating?
- What experiments can you try?

To answer these questions, you need to understand your organization's objectives and challenges. What's keeping your executives up at night? What has them worried about their position? Only then can you brainstorm solutions that fundamentally address their problems.

There is No One-Size-Fits-All Approach

Think of yourself as a doctor treating organizational dysfunction. Your patient (the company) arrives complaining of slow delivery and unhappy customers. You've got options—loads of them! Maybe the cure is better prioritization. Maybe it's eliminating workflow bottlenecks. Maybe it's building stronger stakeholder relationships. Like a good physician, you diagnose first, then prescribe the treatment that fits this specific patient.

Finding Your Strategic Why

Think like a senior executive for a moment. Instead of focusing on daily tasks, ask: *What outcomes am I truly driving for the organization?* Consider these two perspectives:

Output Perspective

- I want to facilitate team events so that the team attends them.

Outcome Perspective

- I want to align competing priorities across business units, so that we can deliver reliable customer value faster and respond quickly to market feedback.

The second perspective focuses on *outcomes*, not *outputs*. It doesn't care about specific team meetings or techniques. Instead, it focuses on delivering value, adapting to change, and aligning organizational priorities.

Your job is to demonstrate how your actions directly contribute to these strategic objectives. Simply put: **stop explaining how you do things. Start showcasing why your work matters to the business.**

This approach shifts the conversation from tactical activities to strategic impact. It positions you as a critical contributor to the organization's success, not just a meeting facilitator.

This is a lot to track. How do I measure outcomes when I'm already stretched so thin?

I hear you. Look, you can't boil the ocean. Start with one relationship, one outcome, and one story where you connect the dots. And then, continue building from there.

Now, how do you figure out what your company truly wants?

Pop Out of Your Team Bubble

Of course, understanding what matters to stakeholders requires building authentic relationships first. When people trust you as their thought partners, they'll let their guard down and be honest about the organizational dysfunctions *they* are seeing—those hidden system-level problems that are holding the company back.

For us to understand what the organization truly wants, we need to intentionally find out (and not just assume). This was one of my earliest mistakes as a delivery change agent. As a fresh-faced newcomer to the scrum master role, I made the inaccurate and ignorant assumption that *everyone* knew who I was, what I did, and what value I brought. (Cocky? Perhaps.)

Had I developed a solid working relationship with Lisa or Kevin (and many others) in advance, I truly doubt those awkward hallway conversations would have ever occurred. But then again, you wouldn't receive the knowledge from my mistakes, so let's consider it a win, yeah?

Time to Create Your People Plan

Let's prevent those difficult "What do you actually do?" conversations by building partnerships that *make your value undeniable*. That's what the "People Plan" is for. This tool identifies the people who can expose hidden organizational problems *and* shows you how to become their indispensable partner.

This template encourages you to think about relationships you may need to build *before* you need them. And trust me, you **will** need them—especially when you're trying to surface organizational dysfunction or navigate complex systemic problems that require influence across multiple departments.

Helpful Tip: Create a separate people plan for each key relationship—one person per page. Think of it as your personal reference file for that relationship—where you track their motivations, personal details, conversation history … basically, everything is in one tidy spot.

Your People Plan	
About Them	
Who is your stakeholder? Julie, Director of Engineering	**What gets them out of bed?** Overcoming challenges, achieving her milestones on time
About You	
What's *your* why? Together, we can efficiently collaborate to solve the sticky challenges the team is facing; I need her buy-in	**What do you want to achieve?** I want to ensure the team has Julie's support and guidance to tackle these technical impediments
Your Plan	
How will you connect? Through one-on-one dialog, maybe we can meet bi-weekly to start	**What action will you take next?** Schedule a casual meet & greet with Julie. Prep my talking points prior to our first call

Here's how it works, and I can't emphasize this enough: you absolutely *must* step outside your cozy little team bubble and build relationships with people beyond your usual circle. I know we love our teams—they're safe, they're comfortable, they're familiar. But here's what I've learned the hard way: **the people who can help you solve the systemic issues aren't the ones moving tasks on the JIRA bard.**

This means looking up and beyond to understand who is in your orbit (their role, influence, status, and perspective) and then discovering what motivates them—what do they fear? Expect? Hope for? What drives their decisions and shapes their priorities?

Beyond your PO and development team, consider connecting with:

- **Senior leadership or executives** who set organizational direction and have the authority to fix systemic problems. When they trust you, you can help them see how competing priorities and misaligned incentives are sabotaging the organization's own goals. (I'm guessing they don't even realize that they're *creating* the very problems that are paralyzing the teams.)
- **Team functional managers** who oversee development, Quality Assurance (QA), and operations. They often hold the shiny keys to making things happen—controlling access to tools, environments, and resources you need. More importantly, they're on the front lines of organizational dysfunction, seeing the competing priorities pulling people in different directions. Pop them on the top of your list because having them in your corner makes *all* the difference.
- **Product leadership** who are consumed with customer value. Partnering with them proves that you're not *just* about processes and guidelines—you care about delivering what matters. These folks see organizational dysfunction from both directions: the strategy churn flowing down from executives and the delivery challenges bubbling up from bewildered teams. And when they see *you* as their ally in delivering value, your strategic worth becomes obvious.
- **People from other departments** such as sales, marketing, and customer support. They see the downstream effects of delivery dysfunction in ways that we never do—customer complaints about missed deadlines, lost deals because of half-assed features, or products that keep evolving. When they trust you, they'll share their own horror stories, which further reinforces the organizational dysfunction you're trying to address.

When you build authentic relationships with these people, your impact becomes visible to senior leadership through team success and stakeholder advocacy.

Next, understand what gets them out of bed.

Think about Jonathan, the eccentric product leader who lives for public recognition, versus Colleen, the QA manager obsessed with groundbreaking testing innovations. Understanding what drives your stakeholders helps you speak their language and reveals why they might be frustrated with current organizational dynamics—exactly the insights you need to solve system-level problems together.

You might not intrinsically know their motivations yet, but you often have a gut feel based on past experiences or observations. Watch for clues: What are their success measures? What gets them excited in meetings? What topics do they repeatedly raise? What wins do they celebrate loudly? What problems make them wince?

If you're new to the organization and don't have enough interactions yet to spot these patterns, just ask directly: "What motivates you?" or "What does success look like for your team?" Having these conversations not only helps you understand your stakeholders, but shows that you care about what matters to them.

Now get clear on your own why: what specific value do you want to create together? Begin with your team. Your purpose here is crystal clear: enable them to deliver value effectively. Now expand that thinking to each stakeholder you listed. For your development manager, maybe you need their support to implement test automation. For your PO's leadership, perhaps you want to improve how business priorities and decisions flow to the team.

For each stakeholder, ask yourself: "Why do I need a relationship with *this person* specifically?" Sure, the ultimate goal is better customer value delivery (this goes without saying), but what can this individual help you with? Maybe you need their influence for buy-in, or you want to understand their challenges better.

Also, remember that relationships are a two-way street. As you consider what you want from each stakeholder, also reflect on what they're likely to want from *you*. What value can *you* provide to *them*? What challenges can you help them overcome? *This mutual understanding* ensures that your partnerships are balanced and sustainable.

Now, get specific about what you want to accomplish. You already know who matters and why each relationship is important. Now define what success looks like. What problems could this person help you solve? What do you want to accomplish here? How will this make your team's life better? And what's in it for the organization?

When you're clear on what you want to achieve with each person, you can build relationships that matter to both of you instead of just networking for networking's sake.

One more thing—and this is important: make sure there's an undeniable thread *connecting your outcomes to the leadership priorities* we discussed earlier. If your CEO prioritizes reducing time to market, partner with the QA manager on test automation to cut release cycles in half. Then later, don't quietly murmur: "We improved test coverage." Instead, specifically highlight the outcomes with enthusiasm: "We reduced release preparation from six days to three days, supporting our goal of faster time-to-market!" This creates that direct line from your partnerships to leadership's priorities.

When your partnerships visibly support what leadership cares about most (faster delivery, revenue growth, and market position) your value becomes undeniable. This alignment is critical; without it, even the best stakeholder relationships won't translate to the organizational impact you're capable of making.

Next, figure out how you'll realistically connect: pick approaches that work for both of you — schedule regular one-on-ones, grab coffee or lunch, connect at company events, and follow up on their town hall topics. Or invite them into team demos, let them observe team events, include them in planning sessions, or share anonymized retrospective insights.

Finally, make it happen: stop planning and start doing. Pick specific actions with real deadlines: Get 15 minutes on Julie's calendar this week. Research her pain points before you meet. Study her recent presentations—what is she excited about?

You've identified your stakeholders, clarified your purpose, set your goals, and planned your approach. Now comes the hard part—*building* these relationships.

This isn't a one-time exercise, by the way. Update your people plan when organizational planning cycles happen, team dynamics shift, new leadership joins, teams reorganize, or priorities change.

This may seem overwhelming—so my advice? Just get started. Identify those critical relationships, understand why they matter, and build them *before* you need them. Trust me—having these partnerships in place changes *everything*.

Why Your Hard Work Looks Like Busy Work

Remember those connect-the-dots activity books from childhood? You'd draw lines between numbered dots, and eventually a picture would emerge.

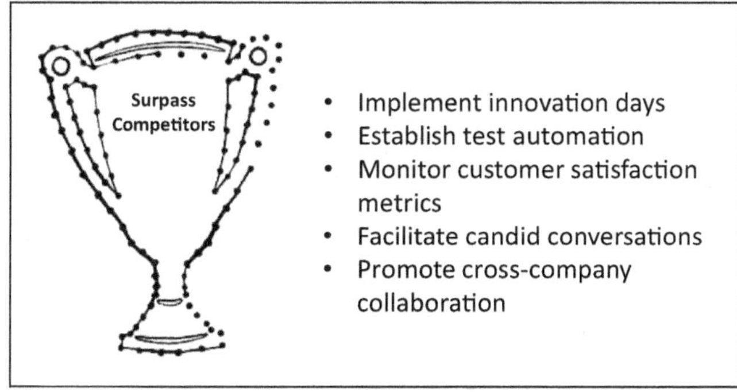

Just as you might not see the trophy until connecting all the dots, leadership might not see how your daily activities contribute to *their* goals without crystal clear connections.

Consider how different these two statements sound: "I manage our delivery process efficiently." versus "I helped our team deliver customer value 30 percent faster!"

The second response connects your actions to business success. But making these connections isn't natural for many delivery change agents—I mean, seriously, who talks like this? Instead, we tend to focus on our activities rather than their business impact.

The people who get recognized and valued *learned* to talk like this. And until the organization understands how our actions drive their goals, they will continue to see delivery change agents as overhead rather than strategic partners.

The key isn't just *gathering* information—it's using it to demonstrate how your role directly impacts business success. What could happen if we reframed the narrative?

Stop Playing the Guessing Game

How do you figure out what keeps your leaders up at night? Just ask. Once you've built those stakeholder relationships, use your conversations to understand what matters most. Ask them directly: What problem seems "unsolvable?" What are **you** being measured against? What's important to you?

And, pay attention during town halls and company meetings. Listen for the pain points leadership keeps mentioning, the metrics they emphasize, the competitors they worry about, and the customer feedback they highlight. These clues reveal what *genuinely matters* to them, not just what they *say* matters.

Then use these insights. Frame your team's achievements in terms of these priorities. Anticipate organizational challenges before they impact your team. Suggest improvements that align with leadership's goals. Focus retrospectives on what matters most to the business.

For example, let's say leadership repeatedly mentions slow time-to-market. You might investigate whether the deployment pipeline is slowing your team down. Or you might talk with the team about how technical debt is reducing their delivery speed, or show data on which practices are impeding delivery time. You could suggest experiments to improve cycle time, spot cross-team dependencies and handoffs that create bottlenecks, or point out how competing priorities fragment focus and delay delivery.

This is how you move from guessing what matters to *knowing*—and that makes all the difference.

Connect the Dots and Take Action

You've learned why delivery change agents struggle to show their value in organizations fixated on visible outputs. You've discovered how to build stakeholder relationships and connect your actions to business outcomes that leadership truly cares about.

The real problem is deeper than individual competence or communication skills. This isn't about you, it isn't about your skills, and it isn't even about your specific role. *This is about an entire category of professionals whose primary focus has been on teams while significant dysfunction festers above us in the system.*

Those organizational blind spots aren't team problems that you can fix with better processes. They're systemic issues that require systemic responses. When you spot these patterns (*and you will*), you're seeing the real reasons projects fail and teams continue to struggle.

The challenge isn't in doing the work (*we know how to do that!*)—it's in **demonstrating how our work drives business outcomes and identifying the organizational dysfunction that feeds the systemic problems**. Like the stage managers in our theater analogy, we create tremendous value that often goes unrecognized. But unlike them, *we can consciously choose* to step into the spotlight.

When you connect with the right people and build authentic relationships, you can surface the root causes of organizational problems and position yourself as a partner in solving them. When you connect your actions to business outcomes, you become the strategic partner leaders rely on for solving gnarly problems.

Here's my challenge for you

Pick just one stakeholder from your people plan and schedule that first conversation this week. Ask them "what keeps you up at night … what problems seem unsolvable … what's valuable to you?" Then truly tune in and listen for how you can help. (Bonus points for repeating back what you heard, in your own words. This helps them feel heard and allows you to seek clarity.)

And as you're building these relationships, keep your radar up for those four blind spots. When you identify competing priorities or knowledge bottlenecks, remember—you're not just seeing team problems, you're seeing organizational dysfunction you can help address. *This* is where you start becoming the go-to person leaders turn to for solving significant problems.

Looking Ahead

You've built the relationships and you understand what leadership cares about. Now what? Let's focus on the area that matters most to every organization: happy customers.

In our next chapter, we'll dive into customer satisfaction—and I'm not talking about tracking dry Net Promoter Scores (NPSs) and calling it a day. You'll learn how to become the person who spots potential issues *before* they happen, turns boring team updates into engaging customer impact stories, and helps solve the systemic problems that created those initial customer headaches.

CHAPTER 3

Customer Crisis—We've Gone From Delight to Damage Control

Picture this: You're in a leadership meeting when the CEO (or some other very important executive) announces, "We have to delight our customers!" As a delivery change agent, you're probably thinking on two levels:

- "How can I help my Product Owner and team tackle this challenge?" (<--Team-level thinking)
- "What could be driving this sudden focus on customer satisfaction?" Or, put another way: "What system-level dysfunction is at play?" (<-- Systems thinking)

That second question is the one that matters because here's what **just** happened: this morning, your executive got an earful from a disgruntled customer, or they saw a competitor's shiny new feature, or the latest NPS scores caused panic and disarray. And although there's an "urgent need to address these issues **immediately**," the irony is that these underlying problems have been there all along. The difference now is that leadership is paying attention.

You Are the Dumpster Fire Spotter

And this is where you can shine. You're not trying to hijack the PO's job—customer relationships are their thing, and you are quite fine with that. But while they're focused on what customers need, you're seeing the organizational dysfunction that's about to create those customer disasters. You are spotting the dumpster fire before it erupts.

But here's where it gets frustrating—spotting the flames early is only half the battle. The real challenge is getting anyone with actual authority to hear you and take action before everything goes up in smoke. I mean, how many times have you seen problems coming and felt completely powerless to prevent them? *This makes you the dumpster fire spotter.*

To get leadership's undivided attention, speak "leader language." Instead of saying "I think we have some process issues," (meek, lifeless) you say "I'm seeing data patterns that are going to create the next customer crisis" (assertive, confident). Your focus is on the organizational dysfunction that's sabotaging customer satisfaction—the stuff they can't see but desperately need to know about.

To get ahead of future executive meltdowns, pay attention to the warning signs. Here are four areas where you can lean in, roll up your sleeves, and dig deep:

- **Support tickets and incidents** (turn these into improvement opportunities).
- **Customer feedback channels** (make sure teams hear the customer's voice).
- **Product usage and performance** (understand what's really working).
- **Market and competition** (know what you're up against).

Your PO probably already has some of this data, which is fantastic. But while they're thinking about what customers want and what to build next, you're digging for the organizational patterns that keep screwing up their customer satisfaction goals. You're looking for the knowledge silos, the misaligned incentives, or the approval processes that are quietly undermining everything they're trying to accomplish. When you dig into each area, you're asking two kinds of questions:

- What's broken right now? (← team level).
- Why does it keep breaking? (← systems level).

The first helps you fix immediate problems. The second helps you prevent future executive meltdowns. **Here are some tips on how to spot the sparks of a dumpster fire, before it ignites:**

Support Tickets and Incidents	Customer Feedback Channels
The team is closest to the code, making you well positioned to help analyze patterns and identify systemic issues.	You can help your product owner connect the dots between different feedback sources and identify organizational barriers to customer responsiveness.
Look at the team: • What patterns do you see across production support tickets? • Which incident types keep recurring, and why? • How quickly are we resolving customer reported defects?	**Look at the team:** • What story are the customer survey results and Net Promoter Scores (NPS) telling us? • What themes are emerging from social media buzz and trending topics? • What patterns do you see in renewal rates and customer retention?
Look up toward the organization: • Are incidents taking longer to resolve because they're being passed between multiple teams? • Which competing priorities are forcing teams to cut corners on quality? • Who actually has the authority to approve urgent fixes when something breaks?	**Look up toward the organization:** • Are customer complaints reaching the teams who can actually fix them? • What gets teams rewarded — working fast or solving customer problems? • Do teams have authority to act on customer insights, or do they require multiple approvals?

Product Usage and Performance	Market and Competition
Partner with your product owner to understand user behavior and identify structural barriers to customer-focused decisions.	Support team discussions by exploring competitive landscape and organizational responsiveness.
Look at the team: • How are customers actually using new features? • Where are we seeing a decline in engagement, and what might be causing it? • What stories do the analytics tells us about user behavior?	**Look at the team:** • What are our competitors offering that we are not? • What market trends should be influencing product decisions? • What customer needs are we hearing from our sales and support teams?
Look up toward the organization: • Are teams building based on customer data or assumptions? • What department priorities are working against customer needs? • How long does it take to go from "we see the problem" to "we're fixing it?"	**Look up toward the organization:** • Are our competitive responses aligned with our actual strategy, or are we just reacting to whatever competitors do? • Do our planning processes reward safe improvements or bold innovation?

Don't just collect this data and file it away for a rainy day. Immediately speak up when you spot these patterns (like support tickets piling up due to competing priorities, or customer feedback that never reaches the right teams). Walk into your next leadership meeting with specific examples in your hand: "I'm seeing three organizational patterns that are creating customer problems. If these aren't addressed, they could escalate." Then lay out what you've discovered.

This two-level thinking is what separates good delivery change agents (them) from great ones (you). You're not just helping teams deliver faster—you're identifying the organizational dysfunction that creates those disgruntled customers in the first place.

Turn Boring Updates Into Customer Stories

At this point, you've identified yourself as the dumpster fire spotter and you know where to dig for warning signs. So, how do you put this into practice? That's simple! Take what you're already doing and add a customer lens to almost everything.

Think about your typical meetings and planning sessions. Yes, you are already guiding clear conversations and debates—that's delivery change agent 101. But what if you pushed further? Instead of asking the team, "How much work do we expect to complete?" (dry, boring, and predictable), try "What customer problems will we attempt to solve?" (thought-provoking, inspiring).

Now, how does the team respond to the rephrased question? What you're really testing is: "do they think in terms of customer problems, or features/technical work?" An indication of the latter is when executives ask "How many features did we ship?" instead of "What customer problems did we solve?" They're signaling that technical output matters more than customer outcomes.

If teams consistently struggle to answer customer-focused questions or default to technical solutions without customer context, **look up**—what organizational signals might be inadvertently encouraging them to think this way?

Here's how this customer lens changes everything, starting with blockers and impediments. You already track and communicate blockers—it's in your DNA. But here's a fun twist on an old favorite: **Frame impediments in customer terms and watch what happens.** Instead of reporting "The application programming interface (API) integration is blocked," (yawn) try "This blocker is affecting a feature that 40 percent of our customers use daily." (oh noooo!)

The secret is defining the "so what?" Keep asking: "How does that impact our customers?" until you get to something that matters. The team says "The API integration is blocked." You ask "So what?" They explain: "Customers are unable to use the search functionality." Keep digging. "How many customers use this? How often?" They admit: "Hmmm, about four out of 10 people search the content daily." Now you've got something. "So, this blocker is affecting a feature that 40 percent of our customers use daily?"

Now here's the systems question to consider: Are these customer-impacting blockers getting resolved faster than technical blockers? If framing impediments in customer terms doesn't change how quickly they get addressed, **look up**—what does that tell you about organizational priorities?

For example, if a blocker affecting 40 percent of daily users still sits in the backlog for weeks while "technical debt cleanup" gets immediate attention, that reveals something about what your organization truly values.

With your demos

We've all been to those demos where the people who primarily matter are nowhere to be found, leaving the team feeling like they're presenting to an empty room. This is because we created one recurring invite and never touched it again.

A product demonstration isn't just a showcase—it's an opportunity to gather insights about whether you're creating happy customers or not. It's also your team's chance to receive (hopefully) positive recognition and feedback. When it's boring and technical? Crickets all around. But when it's engaging and valuable? Standing room only. It's time to rethink who you're inviting and how you're positioning this meeting.

Give your demos a facelift by inviting people who will celebrate and appreciate what they're seeing—the customer support representative who just handled 20 similar requests, the sales team member keeping his ears glued to the competition, your marketing guru who knows what the market is buzzing about, and yes, maybe even some actual customers (gasp!)

Now here's a systems question to consider: If you consistently invite the right people and make demonstrations engaging, but stakeholders still don't show up or don't act on the insights shared, **look up**—what organizational signals might be at play?

Are they measured on attendance at cross-team meetings? Do they get recognition for contributing to product discussions? Or are they so overwhelmed with their own work that attending feels like a luxury they just can't afford? These patterns reveal whether your organization truly values cross-functional collaboration or just talks about it.

With Last Minute Changes

When your team moans and groans about a last-minute requirement change, put a customer spin on it: "This change request came directly from our premier customer's feedback—imagine the praise we will receive when we deliver this!" Welcoming changing requirements, even late in the process, can (and will) boost customer satisfaction.

Now, the systems question: If you consistently frame changes in customer terms but teams "still" resist, what's really driving this? What organizational patterns reward saying "no" to change, even when that change comes from valuable customer feedback? Organizations obsessed with reducing "scope creep" are essentially teaching teams to resist change, even when that change comes from valuable (and timely) customer feedback.

With quality practices

You're already promoting technical practices such as testing, peer reviews, and continuous improvement—that's just standard delivery change agent work. But don't just promote them because they're "best practices." Instead, connect the dots for your team: "Remember those production issues last month that had our support team working nights and weekends? This is how we prevent that from happening again."

And the systems question: If you promote quality practices and connect them to customer impact, but teams still cut corners or leadership prioritizes rapid delivery over quality, what does this reveal about what your organization values versus what it claims to value?

⇧ *Now, Look Up!*

You're doing everything right—framing work in customer terms, inviting the right stakeholders, and promoting quality practices—but organizational patterns keep undermining your efforts. When push comes to shove, does your organization really prioritize customer satisfaction, or does it prioritize hitting deadlines? Here's how to address common dysfunctions when you lack formal authority:

Look Up! Strategies for Making Customer Impact Visible

Problem	Potential Solution
You're hearing "how many features did we ship" instead of "what customer problems did we solve?"	Add customer data to your regular reports alongside the metrics. Stop leading with "completed 5 stories" — try "completed 5 stories, including the search timeout affecting 47% of daily users." Make outcomes visible. Don't wait to be asked.
Customer impacting blockers aren't prioritized over technical blockers.	Lead with the human story. "The mobile app crashes every time users view their transaction history — let me show you." Walk leadership through the embarrassing experience, then follow with data: "Our app store rating dropped from 4.2 to 3.8." (Wait for the mic drop.)
Stakeholders and other key people are consistently skipping the team demos.	Give it a facelift. Rename "sprint review" to "Customer Impact Showcase: See how we solved processing delays!" Frame it as valuable — not an obligatory meeting people feel guilty skipping.
Teams resist mid-cycle change because they're measured on predictability.	Reframe "course correction" as "customer responsiveness." Track teams that respond to customer-driven changes and share their wins, gradually shifting the narrative from "change is bad" to "responsiveness drives success."
Leadership demands speed over quality.	Let the data do the talking. "This week we spent 25% of our time on a bug 2 hours of testing would have caught." No emotion needed — just make the trade-off visible.

You're not reinventing the wheel here—you're just making it roll smoother, faster, and more directly toward customer satisfaction. This also isn't about learning new skills; you're only adding a customer lens to what you already do well.

From Weekend Work to Customer Trust

You can spend months building customer trust and loyalty by delivering useful features, but just one production disaster can destroy it all.

Although new features get customers excited, in reality, reliability is what keeps them around. My friend Josh discovered this when his team's production disasters had leadership questioning everything.

For months, every single release was followed by a storm of failures—system crashes, angry customers, burned-out developers, and stakeholders questioning whether the team could deliver anything reliably. Josh knew he had to do something, but he faced the same challenge most delivery change agents face: how do you fix production issues when you're not the technical expert?

Here's what he figured out: you don't need to be the technical expert. He partnered with people who knew what was broken—the lead developer who understood which metrics mattered, the DevOps engineer who had system stability reports, and the support team tracking customer complaints. He worked with his team to create simple visual representations of all those incidents—line graphs, bar charts, whatever showed the patterns clearly. When technical team members tried to explain what they were seeing, his standing request was: "Talk to me like I'm your grandpa." This rewarded him with the simplified story removed of complex technical details.

Josh made sure the problems couldn't be ignored. He scheduled regular production health reviews with the team, created visual boards showing incidents and their customer impact, and ensured that production issues were part of delivery planning conversations. Most importantly, he connected support teams and developers so they were talking to each other about what was breaking.

Josh didn't need to understand the technical root causes. He focused on what really mattered: how many customers were affected, how long it took to fix things, which incidents kept happening to the same frustrated customers, and what all this chaos was costing in terms of lost revenue and customer satisfaction.

His approach narrowed in on one key question: "Where can we focus 20 percent of our effort to resolve 80 percent of the tickets?" He scheduled weekly meetings with leadership to share what he was finding, and over time, the patterns became obvious to everyone.

And the results were pretty spectacular: Josh and his team reduced production defects by 30 percent—from over 350 to 240. These numbers are impressive, but more importantly, their leadership stopped questioning whether the team could deliver reliable software.

Here's what I learned from Josh—and what you can apply regardless of your technical background: you don't need to be a technical expert to make this kind of difference. Instead of worrying about what you don't know, focus on what you're already pretty damn good at: building solid partnerships, making data visible and accessible, driving meaningful discussions, tracking customer impact, and maintaining persistence in finding solutions.

Josh's approach works because it focuses on the business impact of technical problems, not the technical details themselves. When you translate technical problems into business language—showing the real cost in time, money, and customer relationships—leadership finally understands what's at stake.

⇧ *Now, Look Up!*

You've partnered with experts, collected compelling data, and made everything visible—but production issues keep happening anyway. What organizational patterns are preventing real fixes? And what can you do about it when you don't have formal authority?

OK, let's be honest here—what would genuinely fix this systems constraint is completely outside of your pay grade. Things such as changing performance metrics to reward stability, allocating real budget for technical debt, or making customer satisfaction part of leadership bonuses. Unfortunately, you can't drive these decisions.

So, let's be realistic. As a delivery change agent, you can simply document and expose the business impact through the data: "This quarter we spent 40 percent of our development capacity on fixes that could have been prevented with proper testing." Or "Our biggest client is considering switching providers due to reliability issues." Doing this creates a sense of pressure from outside of development and forces leadership's eyes onto the problem.

And ultimately, if prioritizing speed over stability continues, despite seeing the clear consequences from the data you're providing, you've probably hit the limit of what you can change. **Remember this: expose the opportunity but do not force it.** Sometimes the most valuable thing you can do is recognize when you're swimming upstream rather than working with the organizational currents.

After all, customer satisfaction isn't always about sexy new features—it's about delivering reliable service that customers can count on.

The Band-Aid Addiction

You know what I find so very frustrating? Watching teams repetitively slap Band-Aids on the same problems instead of solving them at the source. When teams only fix symptoms, customers experience the same issues over and over and their trust gets destroyed. What kills me is that teams know they need to dig deeper, but they aren't given the time. So instead, we risk losing customers. Talk about insanity.

I've got good news for you: you don't need deep technical expertise to guide a root cause analysis (RCA); a meeting where teams figure out why problems keep happening. Your facilitation skills and ability to ask the right questions are exactly what teams need to get past surface-level fixes.

When to Jump In

There's a saying: "The best time to plant a tree was 20 years ago. The second-best time is now." The best time for RCA is right after a critical production fix, when the crisis has passed but the pain is still fresh. This is your opportunity to pause and ask: How do we prevent this from happening again?

To develop your RCA radar—the ability to spot when teams are just treating symptoms—watch for these patterns:

- Recurring issues that the team treats as "normal" ("Oh yeah, that happens every release").
- Quick fixes applied without deeper investigation ("No worries, we'll just restart the server").

- Customer complaints that sound awfully familiar ("This sounds a lot like …").
- Team members proclaiming déjà vu during incident discussions ("Didn't we address this last month?").

Getting Buy-In for Root Cause Analysis

Sometimes the biggest challenge isn't conducting the RCA—it's convincing others that it's worth the time investment. How often have you heard "I agree, we should talk about what happened but we don't have the time (energy/bandwidth/resources) for this meeting?" Rather than throwing up your arms in defeat, try taking small simple steps to advocate effectively. Start with presenting solid, unquestionable facts.

- **Document the frequency of similar incidents.** "I noticed that over the past month, we've had five different situations where customers couldn't submit their budget reports. Each time, we fixed it by clearing the cache, but we've never investigated why the cache keeps corrupting. Looking at the data, we've spent about four hours per incident on emergency fixes—that's 20 hours we could have spent on _______ ." (Fill in the blank with something that's important to them)
- **Calculate the time spent on repetitive quick fixes.** "Every Monday morning, we allocate the first hour restarting servers after the weekend batch jobs. We've been doing this for literally years, treating it as business as usual. That's 52 hours annually just on restarts, not counting the delayed start to our actual sprint work."
- **Gather customer impact data from support tickets.** "Looking at our support tickets for our first quarter, 40 percent mentioned slow payment processing. While we've been adding more servers to handle the load, we haven't investigated why the processing is sluggish in the first place."
- **Share stories of customer frustration.** "Our key customer has opened the same search timeout tickets four times this month.

Each time, we've apologized and applied our standard fix, but they're beginning to question why this keeps happening. Our credibility is sliding, which is not a good look."

To level up:

- **Calculate the direct cost of recurring issues.** You could start by tracking the average fix time by the number of incidents. For example, it takes one engineer roughly three hours to fix a production error and we've resolved five this week, we've spent 15 hours (or $3,000—assuming a guesstimate of $200 per engineer hour) on these issues. (Side note: From a tactical point of view, creating tasks is an efficient way of documenting how long it takes to fix an issue. This information will come in handy as you compile the data).
- **Present the impact on the delivery capacity and commitments.** We're not just losing revenue on production defects, but there are direct costs to our delivery cycle. If the engineer's eyes are on fixing incidents, those eyes are not working on committed planned work.
  "Because of these incidents, we had to drop two features from our sprint. Based on our velocity, that's about 15 percent of our time lost to firefighting." Real numbers get real attention.
- **Connect incidents to customer satisfaction metrics.** Partner with your PO to uncover the relationships between the data. "Our NPS scores dropped by five points after that API integration issue, where our customers were unable to use the search functionality."

Once you've successfully made the case for RCA and run a few sessions, create a simple template based on what worked—or feel free to use the following one. Share it with other delivery change agents and refine it based on their feedback. There's no need to reinvent the wheel every time.

Root Cause Analysis (RCA) Template	
Date of RCA/ Participants	July 22, Kevin (VP Engineering), Lisa (Director), Susie (Lead Developer), Casey (QA)
What happened?	Customer demo failed; Application crashed when showing the new reporting feature
When did this happen?/What's the frequency?	During yesterday's quarterly business review, first time with this feature, but 3rd demo failure this quarter
What was the impact?	Lost potential $50K deal, customer is questioning our reliability, the team confidence is shaken
Why did it happen? *(5 Why's)*	1. App crashed 2. Memory leak in reporting code 3. Code wasn't tested with large datasets 4. QA only had access to small test data 5. We don't have production-sized test environment
What evidence supports this?	Error logs showing memory overflow, QA test cases show max 100 records vs. customer's 10,000+ records
What is the solution?	Update staging environment with production-sized data and establish "demo-ready" testing checklist
How will we know the solution worked?	Zero demo failures in next quarter, all features tested with realistic data volumes
Next steps? (Include owner & date due)	Susie: Set up staging environment (Aug 1), Casey: Create demo checklist (Aug 8)

⇧ *Now, Look Up!*

You've made the case for RCA, gathered compelling data, and identified clear root causes—but nothing changes. You've done everything right and you're still hitting a brick wall. What's really preventing action and what can you do about it?

Look Up! Strategies to Uncover the Root Cause

Problem	Potential Solution
Leadership consistently prioritizes new feature delivery over fixing identified root causes.	Present the cost of inactivity in terms they care about (hint: typically, that means in dollar signs). For example, "this issue has cost us 40 hours of development time over three months. That's $8,000 fighting fires that could have been spent on the new client portal." Make the trade-off visible and let leadership choose.
Teams aren't participating in root cause analysis.	Team participation often reflects leadership priorities. If leadership isn't attending or valuing RCAs, team members won't be incentivized to participate either. So, the question is: What's the WIIFM (What's In It For Me?) from leadership's perspective? One option is to try tracking the cost of NOT doing the RCA and present it as a business case. For example: "We've had the same timeout error four times in two months. Each incident takes the team approximately 6 hours to resolve and affects over 200 customers. A 2-hour RCA after the first incident could have prevented 16 hours of firefighting and saved our customer support team from handling 50+ complaints." Framing it in these terms makes a root cause analysis session sound like a strategic advantage, and not process overhead.

RCA is so much more than fixing technical problems—it's about rebuilding customer trust. When teams stop slapping Band-Aids on everything and instead, solve the underlying issues, customers stop experiencing the same frustrations over and over. And when you navigate the organizational dysfunction preventing real fixes, everyone wins: customers get reliable service, teams stop firefighting, and the organization builds a solid reputation for quality.

Channeling Your Inner Annoying Kid

Have you ever participated in or guided an RCA? I'm not going to say it's "easy," but running an effective RCA isn't about technical expertise—it's about asking the right questions and keeping people focused.

- Start with simple techniques like the "Five Whys"—basically, channel your inner annoying kid by asking "why" after every response. Keep digging until you hit gold. Just warn people ahead of time that you'll be doing this, or they'll accuse you of interrogation.
- Use sticky notes and affinity grouping to get everyone's thoughts and find patterns. Work with real stickies or virtual ones.
- Focus on fact-finding, not fault-finding. We want to understand, not point fingers or blame.
- Create a few simple ground rules so people feel safe being honest.

If you're more experienced with facilitation:

- Try advanced techniques like the fishbone diagram (aka: Ishikawa diagram), to visually map out the problem.
- Stack multiple analysis methods on top of each other. Start with something like Liberating Structure's 1-2-4-All for brainstorming, then follow up with a journey map to understand how and when users were impacted.
- Help distinguish symptoms from root causes. A symptom is what you see ("Uh oh. The system just crashed!") while the root cause is what triggered it ("It appears a squirrel chewed through the network cable.") Ask: "What are we seeing?" to identify the symptoms. Ask "Why did it fail?" to find root causes.

Making Sure Something Happens

An RCA is worthless if nothing changes afterward. To invite follow-through:

- **Document the findings and make sure everyone sees them.** If you're doing RCAs regularly, create a simple template so that you're not always starting from scratch every time.

- **Help the team identify quick wins.** Ask: "What's one small thing we can do now that will have the biggest impact?" Assign an owner and a deadline, just like you do in retrospectives.
- **Schedule follow-up discussions.** Otherwise, people forget and nothing changes.

Long-term:

- **Track what gets implemented and whether it works.** Over time, you'll have great stories to share.
- **Make RCA part of your team's regular rhythm.** Build it into your working agreements. On the plus side, you'll have plenty of success stories for your next role.

Now, Look Up!

You're guiding great RCA sessions, documenting findings, and identifying specific improvements—but those recommendations sit in a document gathering dust. Why do action items from RCAs never get implemented? The problem is that teams identify root causes and solutions but are directed to focus on other priorities instead.

This goes back to gathering and presenting data in language that leadership can empathize with. Instead of presenting RCA findings as technical recommendations, frame them as risks: "We've identified three critical improvements from our RCAs this quarter. Based on current trends, we're looking at an estimated 25 percent increase in production incidents if these go unaddressed."

By connecting RCA findings to customer impact and revenue risk, leadership will need to consciously choose between delivering features and preventing customer pain.

If leadership continues directing teams away from implementing RCA findings despite clear business impact data, you've hit the limits of what you can influence without formal authority. Sometimes the most valuable thing you can do is document the known risks rather than invest in prevention.

What Your Metrics Don't Tell You

Oh, how we love our team metrics!

- Velocity guides us in realistically planning how much work the team can achieve based on historical evidence.
- Story completion ratio helps us to understand if the team has a tendency to over- or undercommit.
- Cycle time allows us to identify bottlenecks and improve the process for flow.

But do these, and other comparable metrics, tell the whole story if we're not connecting them to customer value? In my opinion, they're missing the most important piece. I believe that the ultimate measure of business success is delivering value to the customer.

Customer satisfaction **is** your north star—the guiding principle that shapes how you think about all your team metrics and decisions. Team metrics become powerful when they connect to customer value delivery. The customer's experience is what drives the value and impact of the team's work.

- Without customers, there is no product or service.
- Without a product or a service, there is no company.
- Without a company, there is no team.
- Without a team, there is no you.

How can you promote customer-focused metrics? Or a better question is: *should* you? Many delivery professionals worry they're overstepping their boundaries. "Will I be stomping on the Product Owner's toes?" they ask. Nope. **If you're both focused on customer success, you're collaborating, not competing.** Everything we do is for the benefit of our customers.

Also, if your leadership is focused on increasing customer satisfaction, aren't you just a teeny bit curious what the data is saying (if the data could talk)?

Foundation First, Customers Always

Customer satisfaction is your north star—but that doesn't mean it's where you start. If your team can't get features to production, customer satisfaction surveys are the *least* of your worries. You need to build that solid foundation first, while keeping the customer focus as your guiding light. To figure out where your team is now, start by asking yourself these three questions:

- *Is the team completing their sprint commitments?*
- *Is the team delivering working features to production?*
- *Do they have a sustainable pace?*

If the answer to any of these questions is "no," then you shouldn't be worried about customer satisfaction right now. Instead, focus on effective planning practices, addressing team impediments, and improving the development practices and release process. If you answered "yes" to all three, awesome! Here are three more:

- *Is the production environment stable?*
- *Is the team managing technical debt?*
- *Do they have a predictable velocity?*

If the answer to any of *these* is "no," then you also shouldn't be worried about customer satisfaction right now. Instead, focus your efforts on resolving environmental issues, prioritizing technical improvements, and discovering the root cause of that velocity roller coaster.

If you answered "yes" to all six questions, congratulations! Your team has already mastered the basics and achieved stability! Now you're ready to expand your focus to broader customer satisfaction initiatives.

Also, the goal here isn't to become *the* customer satisfaction expert—it's to help your team deliver value. Before pursuing any customer satisfaction initiative, ask yourself:

- Is this the biggest concern for my team right now?
- Will this effort support or distract from our current delivery goals?
- Am I the right person to lead this inquiry, or should I support others who own this space?

Keep in mind, every production incident ticket is a failure in customer experience. Fixing your environmental issues isn't just about team efficiency—it's about preventing the customer pain that comes from unreliable software.

Pursuing Customer Satisfaction

So, you've decided to focus on improving customer satisfaction, but where do you start? It all begins with an inquisitive mind.

Corner your PO, marketing manager, sales people, or customer service representatives to find out exactly *how* customer satisfaction data is being collected and represented today. Common ways to garner customer feedback include sending customer satisfaction surveys, combing through social media chats, reviews, and comments, or calculating resolution rate. What data do you have access to? What is that data telling you?

A popular customer metric is the NPS, which measures satisfaction and loyalty. Customers are asked a single question, typically along the lines of "How likely are you to recommend our products?" or "How likely would you recommend our company to a friend or family member?" with a simple 0 to 10 scoring system (ranging from 0—"Absolutely not!" to 10—"The corporate logo is tattooed on my bicep!").

Based on their answer and number of responses, a NPS score is calculated. The higher the number, the more loyal and satisfied the customer base.

Where to Start the Conversation

Your PO is the voice of the customer, so they're your best bet for understanding customer satisfaction. Even if you've *never* gotten your hands dirty in metrics, you can ask your PO simple questions like:

- "How do you know if our customers are happy?"
- "What type of feedback are you receiving?"
- "Who sees this feedback?"

Does your company use formal surveys or NPS? If so, this is a fascinating space to dig deep:

- "What questions are we asking our customers?"
- "How often do they receive these surveys?"

- "What are we learning?"
- "What actions are we taking to improve the score?"

Or maybe you're comfortable with the data and you're ready to go deeper? Here are other areas to explore:

- How do our scores compare to previous quarters?
- What patterns do we see in the feedback?
- How have we acted on previous responses?
- What changes led to better or worse scores?

Your company isn't capturing customer satisfaction data? That's a real risk that can negatively impact its growth, reputation, and ability to compete in the market. By advocating for customer satisfaction metrics, you are showing leadership that you are thinking beyond just delivery mechanics.

One last thought, customer satisfaction is crucial, but timing is everything. Start where you can make the most impact based on where your team actually is.

Stop Taking Orders, Start Solving the Right Thing

I've noticed an interesting pattern in casual conversations: we talk at length about the what, the how, and the solution. We spend much less time diving into the *why* or the problems we are truly trying to solve. I'm assuming that this is because solving problems is fun! Dissecting, analyzing, or ruminating over them isn't.

This seems to happen *everywhere,* especially in fast-paced environments or solution-driven cultures. We tend to skip the why because:

- We assume that we're already on the same page about the problem.
- We feel pressured to make a decision and move on.
- We avoid challenging one another as its uncomfortable, awkward, or unpleasant.

I'm sure you've experienced this when refining user stories. The PO displays a story explaining what the customer wants and the work the development team needs to do. This is often written from the perspective of the engineer ("As a developer, I want to implement authentication" or "As a developer, I want to integrate the API") and lacks the why. It's missing key elements like the user's need, the business goals, or the outcome behind this work.

This is where you can step in to uncover the why—but first, why does the why even matter? Understanding the 'why' behind the request helps us to:

- Ensure that we're solving the right problem, not just the symptoms.
- Empathize with the customer so that we can discuss solutions that *exceed* their needs.
- Think critically to design the *right* solution rather than the *easy* solution.
- Avoid falling into an "order taker" role—when team members can make their own decisions, they feel ownership and are more likely to experiment and innovate.

The Perspective Shift

Think about those optical illusion images—the ones where you can see two completely different pictures depending on how you look at them.

This famous optical illusion features two overlapping images. It depicts a scowling elderly woman wearing a scarf on her head and a young woman shyly glancing over her shoulder (the old lady's nose doubles as the young woman's jaw). What do you see first in this picture: an old lady or a young woman?

Each time I encounter this drawing, my eyes automatically hone in on the old lady. This could be because I tend to focus on the big picture (and not the smaller details), or my brain associates certain shapes with older people, or it could just be that my eyes naturally gravitate toward the darker lines that stand out from the more delicate lines.

If I were so inclined, I could train my brain to immediately see the young woman. To do this, I would need to deliberately search for her features first, and then over time, my perspective and interpretation would gradually shift.

But once you see one, it's hard to see the other, although both are there, depending on your perspective. Stories written from a developer perspective work the same way. Take this story:

As a developer,
I want to implement authentication,
So that we meet the security requirements.

From what perspective is this story written? Developer (old lady) or end user (young woman)? This story is written from the perspective of a developer—I know that because *the average customer doesn't care about authentication implementation or meeting security requirements.* What they do care about is personal protection, keeping their information safeguarded, and fraud prevention. By shifting the perspective from the developer to the end user, the story looks very different

As a Brightstar customer,
I want my identity to be confirmed upon application login,
So that I can securely access my personal information and prevent unauthorized access to my account.

The first version describes the work the developer needs to do (implement authentication) and why (meet the security requirements). The second version focuses on the user's experience (confirm my identity) and the value they receive (prevent unauthorized access).

When you shift *from the technical how to the business what and why*, the team starts focusing on customer needs, work gets prioritized more effectively, everyone speaks the same language around goals and outcomes, and the team becomes genuinely engaged and motivated.

But what if your PO is *only* focused on the "what?" Maybe they are overwhelmed, stressed about deadlines, or new to the role. Here's what you can try:

- Offer to help prepare stories for the team.
- Develop a simple user story template that includes the "why."
- Focus on the most critical stories first.
- Lead by example (my personal favorite) by simply asking "why?"

Look, I know what you might be thinking: "Kim, my Product Owner isn't going to listen to me about how they write stories. That's not my specialty, it's theirs." I get it. And you're right—you can't force a PO to change how they work.

But here's what I've learned: when you approach this from genuine curiosity rather than criticism, most POs are grateful for the help since they're drowning in their own work too. Frame it as "I'm noticing the team struggles to understand the customer impact—could we experiment with adding that context?" instead of "You're writing stories wrong!" This makes all the difference.

And here's the other thing: As delivery change agents, our enthusiasm for improvement can sometimes barge ahead of our teams' capacity for change. So, keep these three words in mind:

Progress happens gradually

When we embrace this mindset, we create space for sustainable change and build trust with our teams. Plus, gradual progress sticks better than trying to change everything at once.

⇧ *Now, Look Up!*

You've advocated for customer-focused metrics, gathered valuable data, and identified clear problems—but leadership keeps obsessing over delivery metrics instead of customer outcomes. What organizational patterns are preventing this shift? And what can you do when you can't change how leadership measures success?

Look Up! Strategies to Increase Customer Satisfaction

Problem	Potential Solution
Customer satisfaction is not measured at all.	Start small. Partner with whoever typically connects with the customers (sales, support, or marketing) and propose a straightforward experiment: "What if we were to send a quarterly survey to a focused customer segment? With just one simple question?" This could provide valuable baseline data as you work toward understanding customer satisfaction levels. Plus, this feels more manageable rather than overwhelming.
You advocate a focus on customer metrics but leadership only cares about delivery metrics (like velocity and story points).	Connect delivery metrics to customer outcomes in language leadership understands. Instead of presenting customer satisfaction as separate from delivery, show the close relationship: "Our velocity is 35 points per sprint, but our NPS dropped 8 points this quarter. We're delivering fast but we're not delivering value." Make the case that focusing on speed without considering customer impact is like driving fast in the wrong direction.

If leadership keeps rewarding output metrics despite clear evidence that customers are unhappy, consider cutting your losses. At that point, the best thing you can do is protect your team from the organizational dysfunction. Help them understand customer impact even if leadership doesn't care, so *they* can make informed decisions for themselves.

When Curiosity Becomes Interrogation

By nature, I'm an inquisitive human. I enjoy learning unfamiliar skills, discovering unexplored edges, or engaging in profound dialog. My Dad, an unapologetic hoarder of books, magazines, and newspaper articles, was fond of saying "Kim, always remember this: knowledge is power." His wise words clung to me, like a faithful echo, as I progressed through my career. The more I knew, the more adept or resilient I could be.

However, as with most things—my curious nature was a double-edge sword; what I considered to be purely investigative, others have perceived as intrusive, judgmental, or unwelcomed.

Value was always on the top of my mind, so, I tended toward asking a lot of questions (especially during refinement meetings). However, I realized that there's an art to asking questions without disrupting the flow or irritating everyone around me. In my experience, I've learned to:

- **Read the room.** If the PO and the team have a clear understanding, then maybe my questions can be saved for a separate conversation as opposed to keeping the rest of the room held hostage.
- **Look for subtle signs of frustration.** This could include eye rolling (although, that's really not that subtle), bewildered facial expressions, audible sighs, fidgeting, or complete disregard. (Of course, for remote workers, this requires cameras to be turned on.)
- **Recognize when questions are slowing down progress.** If I'm the only one that's finding value in the conversation, that's a pretty good indicator that maybe my line of questioning isn't exactly *adding* value.
- **Avoid asking questions just to be heard.** Early in my career, I thought that to ask questions, (any questions!) was to demonstrate my engagement. I've since learned that my queries should support the team and not impede them.
- **Stay in my lane.** If the value is understood and everyone is aligned, let the team flow. As the delivery change agent, I don't need to be knee deep in the information.

- **Ask questions that help to uncover blind spots.** Questions like: "What assumptions are we making? What customer problem is this solving? What feedback will this elicit?" are all valid questions designed to reveal customer value.
- **Remind myself that I'm there to bridge understanding between the people in the room.** I don't need to be the primary pusher of these discussions.

The biggest lesson I learned was that sometimes the most valuable thing I could do is step back and let the team's natural flow continue without my "imposed help."

Connect the Dots and Take Action

We started with that familiar scenario—leadership announcing "We have to delight our customers!"—and explored how delivery change agents can respond at both the team level and the systems level.

- Team-level thinking: "How can I help my team tackle this?"
- Systems-level thinking: "What organizational dysfunction might be at the root of this problem?"

It's not about choosing one over the other, it's about balancing both simultaneously. You're *already* guiding conversations, navigating blockers, managing demonstrations, and promoting quality. The real breakthrough comes when you shift your perspective **up** to expose those underlying organizational patterns. What we've uncovered goes *way* beyond just team improvements.

- **You're the dumpster fire spotter.** While POs focus on what customers need, you're seeing the organizational dysfunction that's about to create the next disaster. When you dig into support tickets, customer feedback, product usage, and market competition, you're not just gathering data—*you're determining whether your organization truly values reliability or just talks about it.*

- **Production issues are like organizational X-rays.** Josh's story showed us that reducing defects by 30 percent wasn't just about fixing bugs, it was about proving that the organization *could* deliver reliable software. When you can track patterns and ask "Where can we focus 20 percent of our effort to resolve 80 percent of the tickets?" you're uncovering organizational health.
- **RCA reveals systemic truths.** Moving teams from Band-Aid fixes to real problem-solving isn't just about preventing incidents. It's about discovering whether your organization has the appetite for actual solutions or prefers the illusion of quick fixes. (*"Success theater," anyone?*)
- **Data is your BFF.** Throughout this chapter, we've seen how presenting organizational dysfunction through factual data (rather than opinion) creates pressure for change without requiring formal authority. "This quarter we spent 40 percent of our development capacity on fixes that could have been prevented" hits much differently than "We need to focus more on quality."

But here's what ties everything together: *every single team conversation becomes a system check when you know what to look for.* When you advocate for customer-focused conversations but teams consistently resist or leadership doesn't attend demonstrations, *you're uncovering misaligned incentives that no amount of your awesome team coaching can fix.*

When you implement all the "right" practices but production issues persist, customer satisfaction stagnates, or quality suffers, you've probably hit the limits of what your team-level improvements can achieve.

Remember: **Expose the opportunity, but don't force it.** Your job isn't to fix every organizational dysfunction you uncover. It's to make these patterns visible so others can choose whether to address them (or not).

The real power of looking up isn't in solving every systems problem—it's in recognizing when you're swimming upstream versus working *with* organizational currents, and positioning yourself accordingly (*which may mean grabbing a floatie*).

Here's my challenge for you

Start with the foundation first. Ask yourself those six questions: Is your team completing sprint commitments? Delivering working features to production? Do they have a sustainable pace? Is the production environment stable? Is the team managing technical debt? Do you have predictable velocity? If any answer is "no," focus there before diving into customer satisfaction initiatives.

Once you've got that foundation, pick *just one technique* from this chapter and try it this week.

- Reframe one blocker in customer terms.
- Collaborate with your PO/marketing/sales teams to understand how customer satisfaction is measured today.
- Invite one new person to your demo.
- Track one pattern in your support tickets or customer feedback.
- Facilitate an RCA for your next recurring problem.
- Ask your PO: "How do you know if our customers are happy?"

Then notice what happens.

Okay, so we've tackled customer satisfaction—maybe even beating the hell out of it. But what happens when leadership can't comprehend what teams are doing in the first place? You may have heard this leadership phrase before: "I don't know what they are doing." Teams are demoing their work, providing updates, and tracking progress—but somehow, it all ends up in a black hole.

That translation gap (where teams speak tech and leaders think business outcomes) creates its own kind of special dysfunction. When leaders can't see progress, they make bad calls about priorities, people, and scope. Let's fix that visibility problem next.

CHAPTER 4

Status Confusion—Everyone Is Busy, but Nothing Is Getting Done!

I can't tell you how many times I've sat across from frustrated leaders who all say the same thing: "We can't seem to get shit done." So, when a growing real estate software company called us in to talk about their struggles, it felt like déjà vu all over again.

In a cramped conference room, Joe, the CEO of a growing real estate software company, rubbed his temples. "The teams *appear* busy, but I can't tell what's actually getting done."

His leadership team nodded in agreement. Jean, the program manager, added, "When I attend team demos, I find myself lost in technical gibberish. The teams show lines of code, but I can't figure out how it benefits our customers." Dave, the director of product, chimed in, "And I don't see how any of this work aligns to our strategic initiatives."

I've sat in countless meetings where the dialog sounds just like this. Ultimately, I believe that the root of this disconnect lies in a fundamental translation issue.

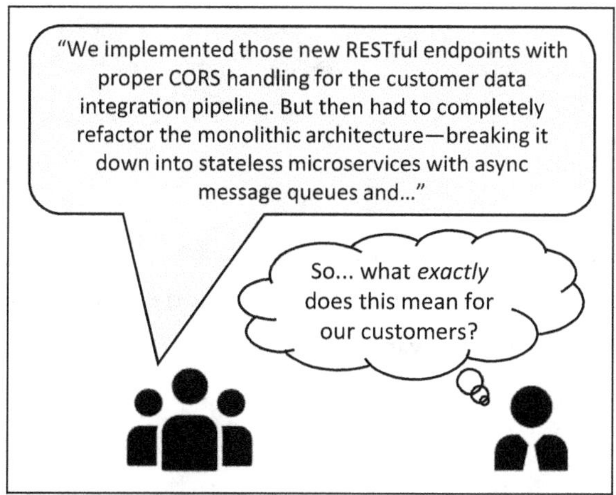

Development teams communicate in "geek speak," while business leaders think in customer outcomes.

It's like they're having two different conversations about the same thing. While teams point to their work boards, daily meetings, and reviews as evidence of transparency, leaders see a wall of technical jargon that obscures real progress. *What feels crystal clear to teams completely confuses leadership.*

Google Translate Can't Fix This Gap

This translation gap starts with *how* teams communicate their work. ***What should be stories about customer value have evolved into dry technical specifications hiding real business impact.***

To put this in context, imagine this: You've arrived at the Mediterranean restaurant your neighbors have been raving about. You slide into your seat and excitedly open the dinner menu. Your eyes scan to the first item listed: "Slow cook protein at precise temperatures in specialized equipment."

Puzzled, you wave the server over and ask, "What is this?" and he says, "Oh, yes! This is a wonderful dish—it's melt-in-your-mouth short ribs with a fig-infused demi-glazed crust."

'Wow, that sounds fantastic' you say, while simultaneously wondering 'why they didn't just *write that* in the menu?' Look, I think we can all agree:

- One version creates confusion, detachment, and irritation.
- The other speaks to value, outcomes, and in this case, your taste buds.

And guess what? *This culture* ***does not*** *emerge by accident.* When teams consistently write "technical menus" as user stories, it's because this particular behavior is being rewarded.

⇧ *Now, Look Up!*

What systemic patterns are encouraging teams to write for developers instead of users? Consider …

- **How teams are rewarded.** Is it through technical complexity or customer value?
- **What leaders are asking.** Is it "how many features were shipped?" or "what customer problems did we solve?"
- **How teams are receiving the requirements.** Are they given marching orders or are they invited to problem-solving sessions?
- **The experience of the POs.** Do they have technical experience or business training?
- **Customer engagement.** How often does the team connect with real users or customers?

Like that dinner menu, the translation gap is just scratching the surface. The real problem goes so much deeper—it's in the organizational systems that inadvertently created this mess in the first place.

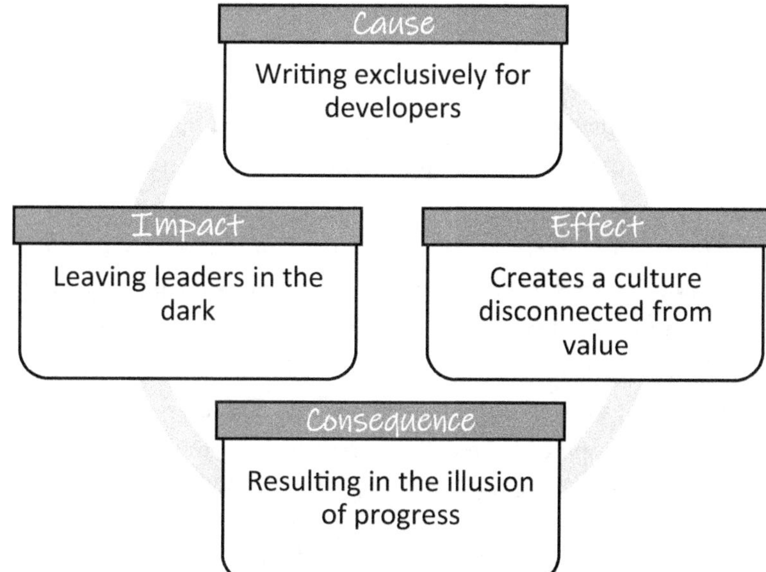

When we write user stories and requirements exclusively for developers instead of users, we create more than just technical documentation—we foster a culture that loses sight of why the work matters.

Where This Translation Gap Shows Up

This disconnect between tech-speak and business impact doesn't just live in user stories—it infects every team event meant to create visibility.

In Your Demos. Let's say you've been working your little butt off building relationships with people outside your team. You've been connecting the team's work to business outcomes, and finally, you're being seen as a thought partner. Then these stakeholders show up to a demo. You feel that spark of anticipation—they're here! They're interested! But as your team dives into technical components using technical language, your stomach drops. None of this resonates. It's just "code-merge-api-endpoint-gibberish." These aren't awkward moments—they're credibility killers.

Teams complete technical work but have nothing a customer can interact with. So, demos either get canceled (suggesting zero progress to leadership) or transform into cryptic presentations that put everyone to sleep. When teams showcase technical components in isolation, it's like a chef proudly presenting individual ramekins of soy sauce, olive oil, and lemon zest that will (eventually) become a steak marinade. Leaders aren't impressed by individual ingredients—they want to lick the finished sauce.

In Your Daily Meetings. Most daily team meetings are (and should be) technical—developers discussing code merges, implementation details, and their strategy for the day. That's their job. The problem isn't the technical discussion itself—it's when leaders or stakeholders sit in on these meetings expecting business updates. For anyone not directly involved in development, these discussions might as well be in a foreign language. When those same leaders glance at work boards filled with stories written as technical specifications rather than user-focused narratives, they can't connect the team's daily work to strategic initiatives. What should be a clear window into progress becomes a concrete wall of technical jargon.

In Your Roadmaps. Have you seen roadmaps that feel more like technical task lists than strategic guides? They promise direction but deliver confusion, filled with implementation details that muddy, rather than clarify the destination. Instead of seeing "Implement batch processing system," leaders need to see user outcomes like "Reduce payroll processing time." One speaks to developer implementation; the other speaks to business value.

Putting yourself in a leader's polished shoes, what they need is straightforward: clear line of sight from their goals to actual delivery, early indicators if work goes off track, ability to make informed decisions about trade-offs, and confidence that teams are focusing on the most valuable work first.

⇧ *Now, Look Up!*

When you see these patterns repeat—demos that showcase components instead of value, daily meetings that sound like code reviews, roadmaps that read like task lists—you're seeing organizational dysfunction, not team failure. What organizational patterns are creating this?

- Are teams measured on "development complete" rather than "customer value delivered?"
- Who creates your roadmaps—and do they focus on technical implementation or business outcomes?
- Do managers reward individual productivity over team collaboration?
- Do people managers attend daily meetings looking for individual productivity updates?
- Are team members split across multiple projects with no "shared work" to discuss?
- Is "looking busy" rewarded over actual progress?
- Are roadmaps created for internal technical planning or external stakeholder communication?
- Does the organization plan in technical milestones (releases, sprints) or business milestones (customer outcomes, revenue goals)?

So, here's the next burning question: how did teams go from writing for users to writing for developers?

The Business Value Murder Mystery

'How did we get here?' This question has been bugging me mercilessly for years. But I don't think there's one simple answer—the shift from writing stories from a business value lens to a technical lens potentially happened due to a combination of things:

- **Skill or training gaps.** Teams never learned how to write user stories properly, so they defaulted to describing what they know and love—the technical stuff.
- **Communication avoidance.** Stories became detailed specifications instead of conversation starters because time wasn't allotted for true business discussions (*Huh? We don't have time for that! Just write down what you need to do*).
- **Planning dysfunction.** Organizations demanded to see every little detail, so technical tasks shapeshifted into stories instead of staying where they belonged—as implementation details that the team managed themselves.
- **Hiring patterns.** POs came from technical backgrounds and never learned to speak business language.
- **Bad metrics.** Teams got rewarded for velocity and story points instead of customer outcomes, so they gamed the system. (*As management expert Eli Goldratt observed, people will behave according to how they're measured.*)
- **Organizational pressure.** Leadership screamed "**deliver faster**!" without defining what was in fact, valuable, so teams skipped the business conversations altogether.
- **Customer distance.** Teams never interacted with actual users, so naturally, they didn't think about them. Instead, they focused on technical requirements and asked POs to write stories in technical terms. POs adapted to meet this need, losing the business value focus.

- **Process obsession.** Teams became more concerned with perfect sprint planning and story point estimation than with understanding what customers essentially needed.

Let me be crystal clear: I'm not saying that technical details don't belong in stories. They absolutely can and often *should* be there! The engineering team needs clarity on technical approach, architecture considerations, and implementation details. Many successful POs include both business value and technical guidance in their stories—usually in a section called "Technical Notes" or "Implementation Details" after the value focused acceptance criteria.

The problem I'm raising isn't about including or excluding technical information—it's when the technical aspects completely overshadow or replace the business value. The best stories maintain both: the clear "why" (that connects to customer value) ***and*** the helpful technical guidance that sets developers up for success.

The Problems Only You Can Spot

So, what's an overloaded delivery change agent to do? Now that you've identified the patterns creating that CEO's visibility problems, you're uniquely positioned to address them. But here's the key: **these visibility problems aren't just *team* issues to fix—they often reveal hidden underlying organizational patterns your company is facing.**

When leaders complain that "we can't see what's getting done," they're not asking for more detailed status reports. They're unintentionally revealing systemic dysfunction that's costing the organization money, reputation, and competitive advantage. You're not just advocating that teams communicate better—you're also surfacing the organizational problems so they can be addressed (*or not, let's keep it real here*). In my experience, visibility problems give you the perfect opportunity to look up:

- When reviews get canceled, it's usually because teams have nothing of value to show.
- When daily meetings parrot verbal code reviews, it could mean the culture rewards looking busy.

- When roadmaps read like a technical task list, it's likely that the organization focuses on the quantity of releases rather than customer value.

What This Means for You

While most leaders only notice the surface-level issues, you can decode what's ostensibly beneath these problems. When they complain about poor visibility, you recognize the organizational patterns likely creating it. This makes you valuable because you don't *just report* problems—you help *address the root causes.*

Sure, I can see these patterns, but I don't have the authority to fix them. I can't change how leadership measures teams or restructure how roadmaps get created.

You're absolutely right. You *can't* fix everything, and that's not what I'm suggesting. What you **can** do is *make these patterns visible*: by documenting them, connecting them to business impact, presenting them in a language that leadership understands. Sometimes that's enough to spark change. Sometimes it's not. ***But exposing the opportunity is your job—forcing the change isn't.*** The key is in knowing the difference.

There's a tool called the onion model that will help you identify and articulate these organizational problems in ways that leadership can't ignore. In the next few sections, you'll learn to leverage this tool and present what you've discovered in language that gets their attention. But, before we go there … Lean in, because this is super important to call out:

Some organizations don't want their dysfunction visible.

(Read that again if you need to.) Fear-based cultures are very real, and if you're the one airing the dirty laundry, you might find yourself on the job hunt. You need to read the room and decide if exposing these patterns is career-limiting or career-building. Sometimes the smartest move is to document what you're seeing privately and use that knowledge to find a healthier organization. Know when to speak up and when to protect yourself.

Because when the culture is right, the goal isn't better team communication—it's making the organizational dysfunction visible so it can be addressed.

The Strategy Misconnection

Let's start with a common leadership refrain: "We know our strategic priorities, but I don't see how teams are delivering on them."

As a delivery change agent, this complaint is your open invitation to investigate. Oooh, a gap between strategic priorities and daily work? That reveals *exactly* where organizational dysfunction lives. But to understand what's creating this disconnect, you need a way to see how work should flow through an organization (the goal state)—and how it realistically does (the current state).

I want you to imagine an onion. Think of its structure—those distinct eye-watering layers wrapped around each other, each supporting the next. In healthy organizations, work should nest inside each other this way:

- Strategic initiatives break down into features.
- Features break down into epics.
- Epics break down into stories.

But here's what I want you to notice: when these layers don't connect, it reveals specific organizational breakdowns. The onion model isn't *just* a planning tool; it's your organizational health dashboard. Each missing or misaligned layer tells you exactly where the system is cracked.

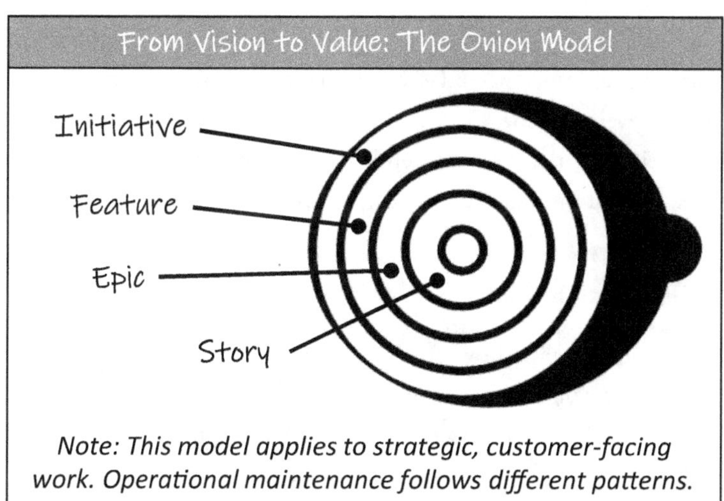

Just like an onion's layers protect and support each other, there's a natural interconnectedness in how value breaks down from big ideas to daily tasks.

Don't get hung up on these specific labels, by the way. Your organization might call these layers "themes," "capabilities," "subinitiatives," or something entirely different that your CTO made up at 2:00 a.m. after too many mocha lattes. The exact terminology doesn't matter—what's important is the concept of breaking down work from big strategic objectives into progressively smaller, more actionable pieces *while maintaining the connection to value.* (If it helps, visualize those wooden Russian nesting dolls.)

Each layer exists to support the core initiative—the strategic "why" behind our work. But to truly understand how these layers connect, we often need to examine them from the smallest unit outward. At each layer, we need to ask: "From a business value perspective, what does 'done' look like in the layer above?"

- The story layer answers the question of "How does the customer know when this *epic* is done?"
- The epic layer answers the same question for features: "How does the customer know when this *feature* is done?"
- And the feature layer answers the question of "How does the customer know when this *initiative* is done?"

What do you notice about the perspective in the above questions? They are framed from the end-user or customer's point of view. Not from Rick the developer's or Cora the architect's perspective. But from the human being on the receiving end, the one benefiting from Rick and Cora's late nights and developing carpal tunnel syndrome.

⇧ *Now, Look Up!*

OK, so you understand how the layers *should* connect, here's what to look for when they don't. When your teams are struggling to connect their daily work to a higher strategy, this is what may be happening:

- **Priority chaos and unclear direction.** This is painfully obvious when you hear phrases like "everything is a high priority!" (they say this jokingly, but trust me, they're not amused). Or you may notice that teams are constantly shifting focus on the newest, shiny object. This indicates that leadership is operating without clear direction.
- **Features are disconnected from the strategy.** When teams are building things that seem logical, but don't support the bigger picture, there's misalignment between product and business. Examples of this include features being chosen based on technical convenience (known as "low hanging fruit") rather than customer value (oh, that's much harder).
- **Vague or unwieldy epics.** No one knows what "done" means for the epic, resulting in work that spans quarters, sometimes years. The cause of this? Organizations plan in stupidly big chunks because they lack either the skills, authority, time, or process to break things down into bite-sized pieces that deliver customer value. (Quick: How do you eat an elephant? One bite at a time.)
- **Stories are written for developers, instead of users.** This is my favorite one, and one we've already discussed in depth. This pattern reveals organizational training gaps, communication avoidance, and distance from the customer.

I want to show you what this looks like when it works, but a brief note before we dive deep: The onion model assumes that you're working with a cross-functional team that can deliver *complete features*—front-end, back-end, the whole thing—*without depending on other teams.*

Also, before you start pounding on my front door—I'm not saying every single story needs to deliver end-to-end customer value. Sometimes you *do* need to build the framework first, and that's perfectly fine. I advise teams to write stories that deliver customer value as often as possible—aiming for about 80 percent. The remaining 20 percent could be infrastructure, frameworks, or technical enablers.

The Onion Model in Action

So, what does the onion model look like in practice? Imagine your company is launching FlavorLab, a food delivery platform that's attempting to do something innovative—inexpensive personalized dining that doesn't suck. FlavorLab's vision is to transform how people discover and order food through three unique features:

- **FlavorLab Match.** AI-powered recommendations that learn what you truly like (not just "you ordered pizza once, so here are 22 other pizza places").
- **FlavorLab Chemistry.** Smart meal pairing that suggests complementary dishes across different restaurants—because sometimes you crave a Dragon roll *and* a spicy beef burrito. FlavorLab doesn't judge.
- **FlavorLab Forward.** Predictive ordering that lets you schedule meals for future-you, from tomorrow's "I'll definitely cook" lunch (*no, you won't*) to next week's dinner party.

Just as you can't launch a platform by simply deploying code and opening the app store, you can't deliver a massive business initiative by jumping straight into technical details.

There needs to be a strategy in place, a deliberate journey that takes us from fanciful idea to grounded reality. Your customer-obsessed leader needs to simplify this ambitious plan—by breaking it into manageable pieces of value that teams can efficiently deliver to the end user.

Start With the Goal (Initiative)

Before focusing on anything else, they would craft their vision—a compelling statement describing FlavorLab's direction and purpose. This is the foundational anchor, the program's core "why," which will be revisited during challenging and stressful times.

In our FlavorLab example, the goal is: "To revolutionize food discovery by creating personalized culinary experiences that delight and inspire." We have now identified the "initiative."

⇧ *Now, Look Up!*

See how this initiative describes a business outcome: "revolutionizing food discovery and creating experiences." It's aspirational, sure, but it's anchored in what matters to the business and ultimately to customers. *That's intentional.*

When you see initiatives that read like "Implement AI recommendation engine" or "Build meal pairing algorithms," you're seeing an organization where technical people are writing the business strategy, when that really should be driven by product/business leaders who understand the customer needs.

Why does this matter? When technical people define strategy, they naturally frame problems through a technical lens. The initiative *then* becomes building impressive technology instead of solving customer pain. Which inadvertently creates: solutions looking for problems … teams building features no one asked for … and everyone working on cool technically sound solutions that completely miss the business goal. Oops.

Identify the Key Areas (Features)

To bring this vision to life, we break it into key customer capabilities, or things **we want the customer to be able to do**:

- Discover and choose restaurants.
- Find and order meal combinations.
- Get food delivered.
- Pay seamlessly.
- Track order status.

Let me ask: Do your features read like this, or do they sound like "Restaurant API integration" and "Payment processing system?" If it's the latter, it's because the technical rot (which started at the initiative level) is already beginning to cascade down.

Determine the Specific Objective for These Key Areas (Epics)

As we contemplate these abovementioned fabulous features, we determine what needs to be done to accomplish each goal. Specific pieces of work (let's call these "epics") under the "Find and order meal combinations" header may include:

- View complementary dishes for my current selection.
- Create a complete paired meal.
- Schedule future meals.
- Save and share my favorite combinations.

Notice the pattern? Each epic describes what the customer wants to accomplish, not how the system delivers it.

Break Down Into Bite-Sized Pieces (Stories)

Next, we deconstruct each epic into specific, actionable, valuable stories. For the "View complementary dishes for my current selection" epic, the stories might include:

- Receive suggested pairings from other restaurants.
- Filter suggestions by cuisine type.
- Filter suggestions by price.
- Mark favorite combinations.
- View flavor profile explanations.

Here's a good rule of thumb—when customer value cascades properly from initiative → features → epics → stories, you get work anyone can understand. If your grandpa can't follow the story, it's probably because the whole initiative was framed as technical work from the start—and that mindset cascaded all the way down.

At the end of the day, we've developed an outline and strategy to achieve our grand vision that may look something like this:

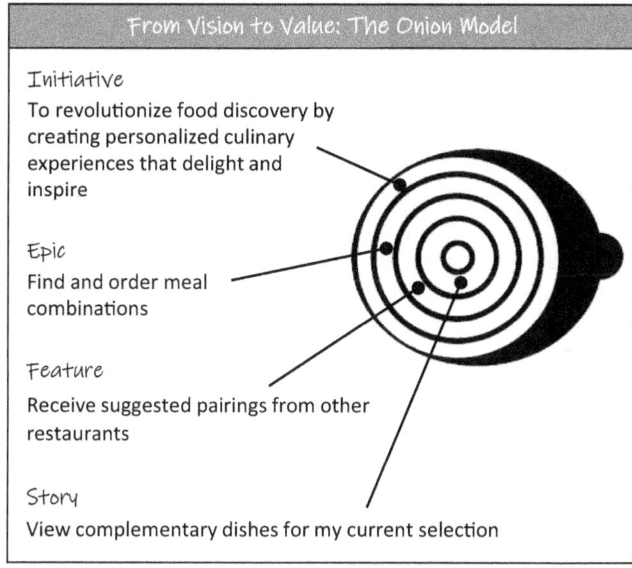

If I were to walk into a meeting room and encounter this delightful onion, I would think: "Check out this company! They've got their act together!"

FlavorLab represents a healthy and aligned organization doing its thing. Every layer connects clearly to the next, the language focuses on customer outcomes, and anyone in the company can understand how their daily work supports the bigger vision. This is not an accident! It reveals an organization where the right people are in the right roles doing what they were hired to do.

Here's another view of the onion model that shows how everything connects across the full initiative.

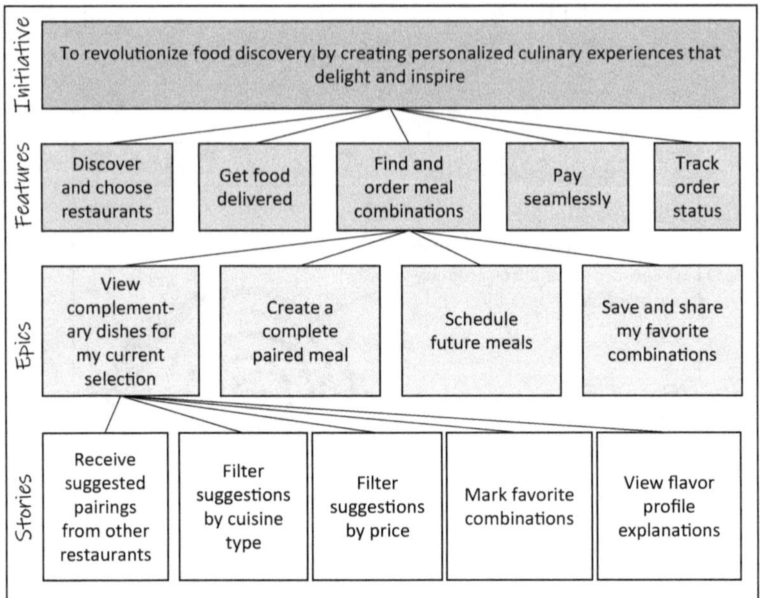

When you see this kind of clear traceability in your organization—where you can follow any story back up through its epic, feature, and initiative—you're seeing strategic alignment. When those connections are missing or unclear, you've found your organizational breakdown points.

When Your Onion Is Rotten

As a delivery change agent, you are *uniquely* positioned to help teams translate their work into business value using this model. But what makes you even *more* valuable is your unobstructed view into the organizational dysfunction that others miss—you see where communication breaks down, where priorities get lost in translation, and where strategic alignment falls apart.

Each moment you're advising teams on the onion model, you're gathering valuable information about what's truly broken. Keep your eyes and ears open for situations like the following:

Look Up! Strategies for When Teams Are Disconnected from Purpose

Problem	Potential Solution
Teams can't explain how their stories connect to epics or features.	This is fixable, but it requires someone to give a damn about context. If you've got the relationship, tell your PO or their manager: "Look, our teams are asking why they're building this stuff because nobody's connecting the dots for them. They feel like order-takers, and that's killing motivation. What if we did quarterly sessions where leadership actually walks them through how their daily work connects to the bigger picture? Show them the initiative → feature → epic flow so they can see their work matters." If you don't have that level of access, become the bridge yourself. Organize one-off conversations where you get leadership to explain the "why" directly to teams. Position it as "helping teams understand the strategy"—most leaders will jump at the chance to share their vision when someone asks.
Stories are poorly defined and rushed through planning.	The best solution is limiting WIP at the initiative, feature, or epic level, but since that requires organizational authority most delivery change agents don't have, here are other approaches you can try: • Provide a visual of all active initiatives, features, or epics across the teams (maybe in the form of a pie chart?) to leadership. Include how long each item has been in-progress and how many teams are touching it, for a much-needed reality check. • Supply specific examples that hit hard: "The mobile app feature has been 'almost done' for 4 months because the teams keep getting pulled into other priorities." • Partner with leadership to break down oversized work. With your guidance, you can help them turn a 6-month epic into 3 smaller ones. • While there, take the opportunity to advocate from MVP approaches. Ask questions that force a thoughtful response: "What's the smallest version of this that delivers customer value?" or "Does the customer absolutely need that in the first release?"
Story priorities are murky.	The ideal solution is executive alignment—either through ruthless prioritization by leadership or a formal governance process (like a PMO) where competing departments ~~battle~~ negotiate over priorities and commit to deliberate decisions. But, since most of us can't create that level of organizational change, here are some more realistic recommendations: • Document and surface the conflicting messages the teams are receiving. This could be in the form of a simple email or in your regular communications with leadership: "The team received three conflicting priorities this week, can we clarify what takes precedence?" The key is having a collaborative energy and raising factual data, so that you don't come across as whiny or accusatory. • Create a simple visual showing competing demands: "Sales wants Feature A by month-end, Product prioritized Feature B, Engineering is focused on technical debt." • Be the courageous one and acknowledge the elephant in the room: "Which project is the most urgent one to complete?"

The solution for all of these? Climb your way **up** the onion model until you find clarity. When stories are unclear, *look up* to examine the epic. When epics are vague, *look up* to the feature. When features don't make sense … well, you know what to do.

Resurrecting Dormant Demos

The patterns you see in demos—whether team's default to technical presentations, stakeholders skip sessions, or reviews get canceled—reveal organizational dysfunction that extends far beyond the teams. When you spot these patterns, you're seeing misaligned incentives, cultural problems, and structural issues—all of which you can do something about:

Look Up! Strategies to Revive Tired Demos

Problem	Potential Solution
Teams showcase technical component s instead of user value.	Structure demos around epic completion, not individual stories. Kick off with a progress update on the epic: "We've completed roughly two-thirds of this epic and expect to wrap up the remainder at the end of the quarter. Let's show you what we've done over the last two weeks." This subtle change shifts the focus from "what tasks were completed?" to "what customer value are we delivering?"
Stakeholders consistently skip demos or appear unengaged.	Coach team members to showcase business impact using "so that" language. "We added batch processing" becomes "We added batch processing so that customers can complete monthly payroll in minutes instead of hours. " This does more than just make value visible—it trains everyone to think in business terms and shows stakeholders that teams understand the strategic purpose.
Reviews get canceled because teams have "nothing to show".	If demos are continually canceled because "there's nothing to show," we know this is probably a larger problem. (Remember the point about work "cascading down?" If the initiative starts out as technical, each layer below that will be infected as well.) The solution is twofold: measure teams based on customer value delivered (not technical milestones completed) and reward collaboration over individual productivity—both of which require a tremendous shift in culture. Which I'm guessing is out of your hands. In lieu of that, you can shine your spotlight on the data by tracking and communicating the patterns you are seeing "We've canceled 3 of our last 5 demos. This equates to six weeks of work our stakeholders haven't seen yet." Another option is to present this problem to the team with the question of "What would need to be different about our planning, so that we always have something to demonstrate?" This question will naturally lead to discussions around vertical slicing.

This is the "look up" mindset in action. Every organizational pattern you identify—from rushed planning to competing priorities to technical work that doesn't deliver value—positions you as someone who understands the concrete problems holding the organization back. You're not just guiding better conversations; you're assessing systemic-level issues that cost the company money, time, and competitive advantage.

Connect the Dots and Take Action

Remember Joe, our frustrated CEO at the real estate software company? His complaint: "The teams appear busy, but I don't know what's actually getting done"—isn't unique. It's a symptom of organizational dysfunction that costs companies millions in misdirected effort, lost opportunities, and strategic confusion.

Here's what we've discovered so far: **visibility problems aren't team problems, they're organizational problems**. When teams communicate in technical jargon ... when demos get canceled ... when strategy doesn't connect to daily work, you're witnessing the result of misaligned incentives, poor measurement systems, and structural barriers that no amount of better meeting facilitation can fix.

The onion model isn't just a planning tool—it's your organizational health dashboard. Each missing or misaligned layer tells you exactly where the system is cracked and leaking. When you see initiatives written in geek speak ("implement AI recommendation engine") instead of customer outcomes ("provide new food recommendations"), you're spotting a very real organizational dysfunction where technical people are defining customer value.

When teams consistently write stories like "Create database schema" instead of "Receive suggestions that complement my selection," you're seeing the translation gap that hides business value from leadership. This isn't a team writing problem—it's a symptom of organizational patterns that reward technical output over customer outcomes.

What This Means for You

You're uniquely positioned to spot these organizational patterns because you see what others miss:

- You recognize when teams can't explain the "why" behind the "how," revealing a disconnect between product and technology.
- You notice when competing priorities cause teams to spin because clear direction is missing.
- You identify when demos become irrelevant because the organization rewards activity over outcomes.

Every pattern you identify—whether it's canceled demos, technical stories, or stakeholder disengagement—reveals something specific about how your organization operates versus how it *claims* to operate.

Your Strategic Advantage

This ability to spot patterns is what makes you a strategic partner. You're not just helping teams run better—you're uncovering the real reasons things go wrong and showing leadership what needs to change.

- When you show leadership that canceled demos represent six weeks of work nobody validated, you're showing them real risk.
- When you connect technical stories to strategy problems, you're explaining why projects fail.
- When you track the cost of competing priorities, you're building the case for change.

Here's my challenge for you

Are you ready to start identifying what's *truly* going on in your organization?

Target	Challenge
This Month	• **Attend one team demo** and note what gets showcased—technical components or customer value? • **Truly listen to your next daily meeting**—are teams discussing strategy or just status updates? • **Review three recent user stories**—how would you explain the customer benefit to a nontechnical friend in simple terms?
This Quarter	• **Track the frequency of canceled demos** (including the justification). • **Document competing priority messages** teams are receiving. • **Map one epic using the onion model**—can you track stories back up to the initiative?
This Year	• **Present one example of organizational dysfunction with data** (canceled demos, competing priorities, etc.). • **Facilitate a robust conversation between leadership and teams**—focusing on the "why" behind the work. • Partner with your product owner to **reframe a technical roadmap in customer terms.**

Remember: Start small and pick the pattern that's most apparent. You don't need to identify everything at once—just make one problem visible and build from there.

Also? You can't fix every problem you find—that's not your mission. But you *can* make these problems visible so leadership can decide what to do about them. Because sometimes the most valuable thing you can do is simply help an organization see what's really happening.

Once you make work visible and connect it to the strategy, you often discover something else that's been swept hastily under the rug: productivity drains that are *sucking the life out of the organization*. Things like unplanned work (derailing every sprint), excessive WIP (creating the illusion of progress), and priority churn (leaving everyone exhausted and in disarray).

CHAPTER 5

Resource Waste—We Are Bleeding Money at an Alarming Rate

Those productivity drains I just mentioned—the unplanned work derailing sprints, the excessive WIP creating illusions of progress, the priority churn exhausting everyone—they are **pricey**. And dangerous, because most organizations can't see them.

When pressure mounts to improve efficiency, the focus often turns to "resources" (and by resources, they mean *people*, not office furniture). But before organizations start eliminating roles or restructuring teams, let's look at something that often goes unnoticed: "the waste" hiding in plain sight.

As a delivery change agent, you notice what others miss. Leadership sees struggling teams and assumes that the problem is speed or talent. You recognize the organizational patterns *creating* that struggle in the first place.

Waste is just that: work that consumes time, effort, and money without adding value. Think about your day so far—how much time have you spent in meetings that could have been e-mails, waiting for approvals that *shouldn't need* approval, or untangling processes that should be relatively simple? It's these unnecessary meetings, endless e-mail chains, confusing processes, and redundant tasks that eat away at productivity while masquerading as "business as usual."

While we can easily track obvious costs like salaries and tools, the most expensive waste often goes completely unnoticed. I'm sure you're familiar with these three classics:

- The constant stream of unplanned requests that shatters focus and motivation (*surprise!*).

- The overwhelming (and growing) pile of WIP that never seems to get done.
- The inability to prioritize, leading to overcommitment and broken promises.

But here's what most people miss: **these aren't just team problems to fix with tighter processes.** They're symptoms of organizational issues—unclear boundaries, competing goals, and misaligned incentives. And when left unchecked, they lead to:

- **Technical debt** as corners are cut to maintain pace.
- **Burnout** as team members work longer hours to compensate.
- **Quality issues** that create even more work.
- **Growing frustration** that pushes high performers to leave.
- **A damaged reputation** from broken delivery promises.

Let's dig into where this waste intrinsically lives—and what you can do about it.

The Six-Gallon Problem

Software development is *expensive*. While we can easily track costs like yearly salaries, tool licenses, and overhead (lights, facilities), some of the more critical costs are harder to spot—like the price we pay for saying "yes" to unplanned work *while maintaining our existing commitments.*

What exactly is unplanned work? It's any research request, urgent requirement, high priority production defect, enhancement, or other task that arrives after the team has already made their commitments. You may have also heard this referred to as "churn," for good reason as it agitates everything: first the plan, then the team members themselves.

To be clear, it's not the *request* itself that hurts us—it's our natural instinct to enthusiastically accommodate that extra work **on top** of everything else we have committed to do. This tendency to say "yes" ignores one simple truth: **we have limited capacity.**

But what most of us overlook is that constant unplanned work isn't just a *team* time management problem—it's usually a symptom of organizational dysfunction. No clear decision-making authority (who has the final word?). Competing departmental priorities (whose priorities win?). No shared definition of what exactly constitutes a real emergency (if everything is an emergency, is *anything* an emergency?).

For s's and g's (that's shits and giggles), let's compare a team's capacity to a bucket of paint.

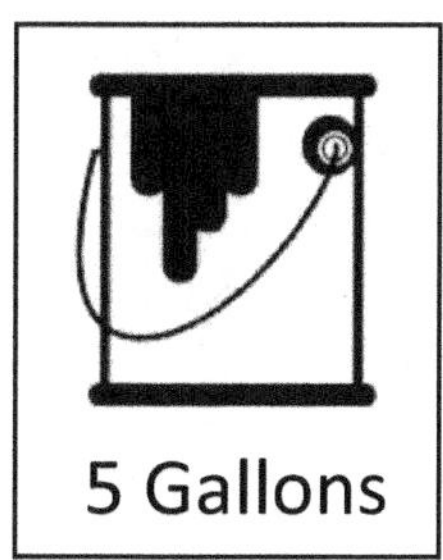

If this can represents our team capacity, it holds exactly five gallons. What happens when we pour in six gallons of liquid? It overflows, making a mess. If the can is made of cheap plastic, it might even split open, spilling everything. What it won't do is magically expand to fit the extra paint. Because that's not how physics works.

This capacity problem is universal, whether we're talking about paint can sizes, highways at rush hour, or team velocity. *There is always a limit.*

To better understand the hidden costs of accepting unplanned work into an already packed iteration, let's visit Softdev Solutions, a fictional software development company. Here, your team builds dental practice software and has committed to reducing new patient setup time from 2 hours to 15 minutes by the end of the sprint.

Today is the Monday morning daily meeting, and you notice Kyle, one of your most reliable team members, hasn't made any progress since Friday. When asked why, he explains that Danielle, the CTO, surprised him in the break room last week with an urgent request—to tighten up the user interface (UI) before next week's board meeting.

Look, we've all been there: someone with authority asks for our help, and suddenly our carefully planned day gets derailed. (My husband Eric calls this the "ole swoop and poop"—picture a seagull swooping in, dropping a mess, and flying away.) Kyle, like most of us would, set aside his sprint work to fulfill the CTO's design requirement. After all, we've been taught to "welcome changing requirements, even late in development."

But, and here's the catch, there's a crucial difference between embracing change and blindly saying yes to everything.

Embracing change means being adaptable and responsive to shifting business needs. **But it doesn't mean dropping *everything* to chase all the special requests that come our way.** True agility requires making informed decisions about what work to take on and what to defer, understanding the real costs of each undertaking.

So, what did this UI distraction fundamentally cost? Beyond the obvious time spent making the changes, there's a hidden expense most people miss.

The Context Switch Tax

What is "context switching?" Context switching happens when you shift focus between different tasks. While it might not seem like a big deal to redirect from feature development to UI design, it actually is. Because the hard work happens when your brain struggles to reload all the details and requirements needed for the new task.

For developers, swapping tasks means Kyle has to remember the *exact status* of multiple features in different stages of development: which database queries were optimized, which API endpoints still need error handling, or what specific business logic was being implemented. When Kyle switches from the UI design work back to the patient onboarding feature, he needs time to remember where he was in the code, what he was trying to accomplish, and how different parts of the system work together.

Let's do some simple math to calculate the actual cost of this unplanned request, assuming Kyle's time is worth $100 an hour.

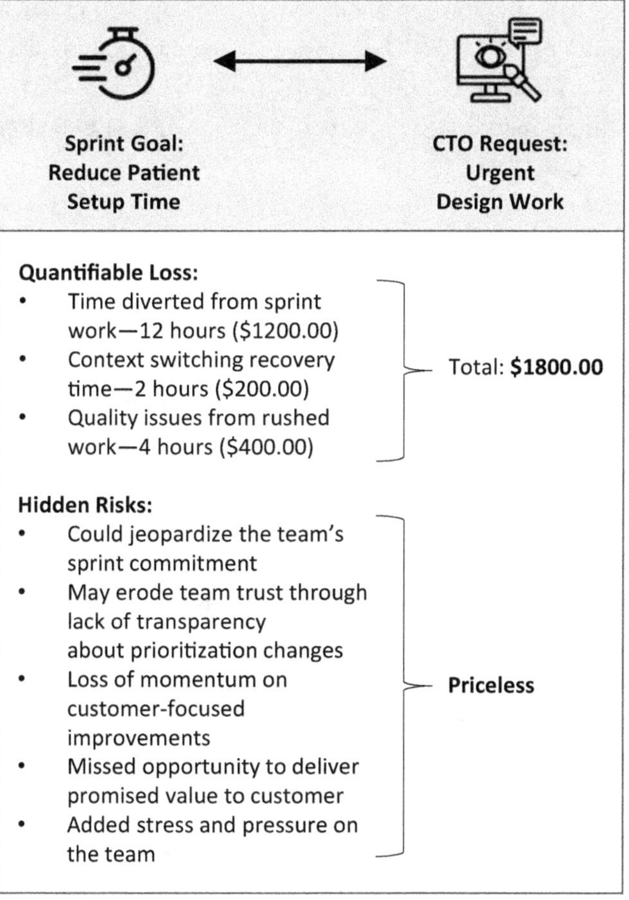

Diagram showing competing priorities (Sprint Goal versus CTO Request) with quantified costs and hidden risks of context switching.

Calculating the Direct Costs

First, there's the time diverted from sprint work. Kyle spent 12 hours on UI design, which translates to $1,200 in lost development costs. But that's just the obvious part.

When Kyle switched from the committed feature to the UI and back again, he lost two hours ($200) rebuilding his mental context. Even small amounts of lost focus time add up quickly—turning a hasty design request into a much more expensive proposition than it initially appears.

Then there's the quality fallout. Kyle's rushed work to catch up on sprint commitments introduced bugs that required four hours of fixes and additional testing—another $400.

That unplanned design work cost the company $1,800. But there's even more to the story.

Understanding the Sneaky Impacts

This situation rippled through Softdev Solutions in several ways:

- **The team's sprint commitment was jeopardized.** Kyle's unexpected reassignment cost the team a critical day of development, threatening their promise to reduce patient setup time.
- **Team trust was eroded.** Kyle's failure to communicate the priority shift left his team members wondering why sprint progress suddenly stopped.
- **Momentum was lost.** By refocusing his attention, brain power, and time on an unrelated item, Kyle's flow was disrupted, leading to a decrease in productivity and an increase in errors.
- **Risks remained hidden.** Because the team wasn't informed about the priority change, they couldn't assess the risk or adjust their plans accordingly.

- **Hierarchy overrode healthy practices.** When Danielle made her request, Kyle felt he couldn't disappoint the CTO by refusing or suggesting that the proper channels be followed, so he took on the work—no questions asked.
- **Consequences remain neglected.** Danielle made her request without understanding the scope, time, or impact on the team's sprint commitments.

Now, Look Up!

Kyle's situation isn't unique—it reveals extremely common organizational patterns:

- Leadership bypasses established team processes, which indicates a disregard (intentional or not) around team commitments.
- This hierarchy prevents people from following normal change procedures, thus rewarding authority over healthy practices.

These aren't "Kyle" problems or "team" problems—they're system problems that create these undesirable situations.

What would you do?

In the abovementioned scenario, how would you have proceeded after learning about Danielle's request to Kyle?

(a) There's nothing I need to do, what's done is done and we can't turn back time.
(b) Look, Kyle should have talked with the PO directly. This is on them.
(c) Why are we even having this conversation? I don't see the problem since it's our responsibility to do what's being asked. *Especially,* if it's the CTO doing the asking.

(d) As a team, we should take the opportunity to inspect this scenario and discuss the path forward should this reoccur.
(e) Excuse me while I burst, Kool-Aid man style, into Danielle's office to demand that she leave Kyle and the team alone.

For this particular scenario, "D" is the optimal answer and since it's fresh on everyone's minds, now would be the perfect time to discuss what Kyle encountered and how this sticky situation could be handled in the future.

Your Ambush Defense Strategy

So how do you help your team handle this better next time? The key is framing the conversation so nobody feels like they're on trial. You want collective problem-solving, not one team member getting roasted in front of everyone. Compare these approaches:

- Individual focus: "Kyle, what was the impact of *your* choice? What options might *you* have had?" versus
- Team focus: "What was the impact of *our* choice? What other options might *we* have had?"

The first approach could put Kyle on the defensive, while the second invites the entire team to learn and problem-solve together. When I'm facilitating these discussions, I lean on questions like "Can you help us understand the situation?" or "What were the factors influencing our response?" or "What other options might we have had?" Notice how each one invites the *whole* team into problem-solving rather than putting Kyle on trial.

By phrasing questions in this way, we avoid singling out individuals and instead create shared accountability for both the problem and its solution. These discussions also reveal organizational dysfunction if you know what to listen for:

Words Spoken	Pattern	The Optimal Fix	A More Realistic Fix
"We don't say no to the CTO!"	**Hierarchy Overrides Team Commitments**	• Leadership held accountable for respecting team processes • Clear rules about when teams can be interrupted and by whom, with adherence to these boundaries • Shift the culture: leaders model respect for team commitments instead of creating false emergencies	• Document and communicate the business impact in concrete terms. "This request cost us 8 hours and put our commitments at risk." • Make the pattern visible through data so leaders see the undeniable cost of their "quick asks"
"We didn't know who to ask."	**Unclear Authority Structures**	• Simple decision - making structure in place with defined roles and responsibilities • Published escalation paths that leadership models • Defined criteria for what constitutes a *real* emergency, with actual enforcement	• Partner with your PO and their manager to create a simple decision tree. "When urgent requests come in, here's who makes the call." Make it visible and socialize it • Take it one step further by documenting when the decision tree gets bypassed (to help illustrate the pattern)
"This happen s all the time."	**Systemic Pattern Ignored**	• Leadership encourages teams to have dedicated time for root cause analysis and implementing solutions • Organizations prioritize solving recurring problems at their source rather than firefighting • The overall culture prides themselves on prioritizing prevention over reaction	• Showcase the team's brutal reality by placing the data front and center. "We've had 7 unplanned requests in 3 sprints, costing us 30% capacity." • Insist your PO builds interrupt capacity into planning; 20% is a good number to start with

Having these insights help you understand whether this is a one-off situation or a systemic pattern. And when you spot systemic patterns, you can decide whether to address them with leadership or just help your team navigate the dysfunction on their own.

Helpful Tip: When asking open questions, let the team answer them!

I know that sounds obvious, but I've witnessed too many provocative (not "sexy" provocative, more like "profound" provocative) questions get buried under rapid-fire follow-ups:

What other options might we have had? (waits a millisecond) *Could we have talked to the PO? Could we have asked about the deadline? Could we have found someone else to help?*

When you immediately offer multiple choice answers, you're undermining your team's intelligence and creativity. I know that's not your intent, however, you're inadvertently sending a message that you don't trust them to come up with viable responses on their own. You've effectively killed the conversation before it had a chance to begin!

Instead, ask the question, pause, and wait. Resist the urge to offer a lifeline (silently count to 10 if you have to). Yes, the stillness may feel uncomfortable, but the team's thoughtful and insightful answers might surprise (and even inspire) you!

When to Step in, When to Step Back

In our Softdev Solutions example, the situation occurred in the past. But what if you had overheard Danielle (the CTO) speaking to Kyle (the developer) in the breakroom, in real time? As a delivery change agent, you may find opportunities to help the team navigate the tension between maintaining focus and responding to business needs.

When you witness these requests happening, your first move could be respectful intervention. One option is to politely interrupt the dialog between Danielle and Kyle, from a curious and objective perspective: "I apologize for intruding, but I overheard your conversation. Let's pull the Product Owner in so we can discuss how to strategize or reprioritize our sprint work, in order to meet this new request." This is just a conversation starter. From here, you might:

- Get curious about what problem Danielle is essentially trying to solve (maybe there's an easier fix).
- Help her understand how this impacts what the team already committed to.

- Pull in other stakeholders to make an intentional prioritization decision.
- Use this as a chance to establish better protocols for next time.

Keep assuming positive intent from Danielle's perspective. The goal is to help the team meet their commitments while maintaining positive stakeholder relationships.

A secondary approach would be to reach out to the PO, prior to engaging with Danielle. While you may not be formally responsible for the team's focus, you're often well-positioned to ensure the appropriate people are aware of what's transpiring behind the curtain. Explain Danielle's request along with the potential implications or impact to the project and wait for the PO's reaction.

If intervention doesn't work, let natural consequences take over

If your interventions aren't working—if stakeholders keep bypassing processes, if teams keep saying yes despite your guidance or pleas—sometimes the most valuable thing you can do is step back, grab some popcorn, and watch the action play out.

Whether it's the CTO, the employee's direct manager, the loudest stakeholder, or a colleague making the request—there will *always* be pressures on the team's commitments. My first instinct was to jump in and shield the team from these disruptions ("look at me, I'm saving the day!"). But experience has taught me that sometimes the team *needs* to feel the impact of taking on too much work to truly understand why focus matters.

Letting teams feel the consequences of overcommitment teaches them *way more* than protecting them from it *ever* could. When they experience the stress, the missed commitments, and the quality issues that come from saying yes to everything, they develop their own boundaries organically. (And you're saved from looking like the bad guy. Bonus!)

Finding the Balance

I'm not saying to abandon your team. It's about recognizing when intervention is helpful versus when natural repercussions are the better teacher. Start with respectful intervention, but don't exhaust yourself trying to protect teams from every poor decision—especially when those decisions might be the exact lesson they need to learn.

Conquering the Interruption Tsunami

Have you ever been so absorbed in work that you lose track of time? The world fades away, you're in the zone, and everything just clicks? That's flow—that magical state where you're fully present and solutions come effortlessly.

And then it happens—a "quick question" breaks your concentration. Or an "urgent request" pulls you into an impromptu meeting. Just like that, the flow is gone, and with it the momentum that was carrying you toward something great. Each interruption doesn't just pause your work—it shatters your focus and forces your brain to rebuild its entire context.

Take Kyle's case from our software company example: his "quick" switch to UI design didn't just delay one sprint story—it cost him his momentum, focus, and efficiency, resulting in a cascade of delays. This happens **all the time** in software development: an urgent bug fix, a hurried research request, or an unexpected plea from leadership that "won't take long." While each unplanned item might seem minor, the cost is far greater than most organizations realize.

As a delivery change agent, you have a unique opportunity to help the team protect their flow without becoming the "Department of No." Here are a few strategies for handling interruptions:

- **Advocate for clear boundaries.** Work with your PO and team to establish boundaries around when and how to engage the team for *truly urgent matters*. "What exactly is 'truly urgent'?" you may be wondering. Solid question! This is where you can help the team advocate for defining:

- what constitutes a *real* emergency (and what doesn't);
- who has the authority to interrupt sprint work with the urgent request;
- how requests get communicated and evaluated; and
- what information is needed to assess the impact.

- **Push for visibility of unplanned work.** Whether you note it directly or advocate for better tracking, help make interruptions visible to stakeholders. When that "straightforward bug fix" turns into six hours of lost development time, having the data helps drive improved decisions. Encourage capturing both the direct time and the hidden recovery costs.
- **Champion for an "unplanned work" story in each iteration.** Partner with your PO to log surprise requests in a dedicated story. By tracking this data over several sprints, you may discover that approximately 20 percent of the team's time goes to handling urgent unexpected requests. Armed with this insight, you can help the team make the case for planning sprints at 80 percent capacity, leaving a buffer for those inevitable surprises. This simple change could help them consistently meet their sprint commitments despite the unplanned work.
- **Propose the "one in, one out" (OI-OO) rule.** Owing to limited closet space, I've incorporated a personal rule where one pair of shoes purchased equals one pair of shoes donated (trust me, it's an agonizing decision). Consider suggesting this approach to your team: when truly urgent work arrives, remove a lower priority item of equivalent effort. This helps preserve capacity and forces conscious trade-off decisions.

⇧ *Now, Look Up!*

Most organizations don't even track the direct time spent on interruptions, let alone the *hidden costs*: the time to regain focus, rebuild mental context, and recover momentum. This systematic blind spot leads to significant underestimation of interruption impact. As a delivery change agent, you can drive real change in three ways:

- **Establish explicit interrupt boundaries with leadership.** Partner with managers and POs to create and enforce clear criteria for what constitutes a **true** emergency. For example: "If it's not truly urgent enough to wake someone at 3:11 a.m., it can wait for the next planning cycle." (Tip! Add this rule to the team's working agreements for future accountability.)
- **Build stakeholder education programs.** Facilitate training sessions that help leadership understand the true cost of context switching, using the data you've been compiling to make the impact visceral and personal.
- **Make interruption costs visible in leadership reporting.** Propose adding "unplanned work impact" to reviews or leadership dashboards so the volume, impact, and pattern become impossible to ignore. This could look something like: "Unplanned Work This Sprint: 18 hours (22 percent of capacity)" or "Sprint commitment reduced from five stories to three due to interruptions" or "This is the fourth sprint where unplanned work exceeded 20 percent."

Stopping the Context Switch Madness

By helping the team remain focused, I've found a few ways to reduce the mental cost of task switching:

Advocate for stacked meetings. Suggest scheduling meetings consecutively—like the daily catch up from 9:15 to 9:30 followed immediately by story refinement from 9:30 to 10:30. This combines their meeting time into one larger block, leaving the rest of the day free for deep work and maintaining flow.

Work with your team to establish scheduled "focus time." Help coordinate specific recurring hours or days where the team commits to uninterrupted work. Some teams use techniques like "No Meeting Wednesdays" or core focus hours where interruptions are strongly discouraged.

Advocate for "I'm in focus mode" signals. Support establishing indicators for when someone drops into deep work mode unexpectedly. For colocated teams, simple physical signals work well. I know a developer who attached a sign on the back of his chair that read "unless it is an emergency, please send an e-mail"—and it worked beautifully. Nobody interrupted him (or even sent e-mails!). In today's remote world, teams can take advantage of virtual tools by setting Teams or Slack to "Do Not Disturb" to protect their focus time.

Champion the goal of completing one task before starting another. Consider sharing the concept "Stop Starting! Start Finishing!" to remind people that every in-progress item ties up mental energy and team capacity. Teams that embrace this mindset often see improved focus and flow.

One caveat to this: As my mentor David points out, this doesn't mean that natural pauses can't be used productively. As a developer, he would use the time spent compiling code to think through and refine future sprint work, which helped his team be better prepared. The key is distinguishing between productive use of downtime and actively juggling multiple development tasks.

⇧ *Now, Look Up!*

Leadership needs these focus strategies too! These folks are frequently attending back-to-back meetings, interrupting teams with "quick questions," and jumping between priorities, thus modeling the *exact behavior* that destroys flow. In this case, their own. As a delivery change agent, you can help leadership break these patterns:

Promote more sensible meeting schedules. When you see leaders scheduling scattered check-ins throughout the week, suggest packaging them: "What if all of your team touchpoints were moved to Tuesdays? That would free up solid blocks of focus time for the teams *and* for you."

Politely circumvent the interruptions. When leaders ignore focus signals or barge into the team's slated "heads down" time, don't hesitate to respectfully redirect: "The team is in their flow mode until 4:00 p.m. Would you like me to grab you then for a brief chat?"

Hold up the mirror. When leaders are juggling multiple priorities, use questions to create awareness: *What could success look like if we focused our energy on completing Project A before diving into Project B?* This question helps them see what laser focus *could* realistically deliver.

Remember: While we can't eliminate all context switching, we can get smarter about handling it at both the team and leadership levels. Everyone's productivity (and sanity) will thank you for it.

	Day 1		
	Ready	**In Progress**	**Done**
Dusty	Story Story Story Story Story Story	Story Story Story	
Chase		Story Story Story	
Kyle		Story Story Story	
Karissa		Story Story Story	
Casey		Story Story Story	
Laurel		Story Story Story	

The Starting Addiction

Back at Softdev Solutions, you notice a (let's call it "interesting") pattern: each team member has started working on three different stories simultaneously.

Based on historical sprints, you know it takes one person roughly three days to complete a single story. So, tell me—what is your initial reaction to the team's day one strategy?

Perhaps you are chuckling to yourself because you've been down this path before (and have an idea of what's to come). Or maybe you are leaning into curiosity, wondering what the team's approach is, or why this strategy may be misguided. Or perhaps, you're thinking "This is fine. Why are you insinuating this is a problem?"

Taking it a step further, if you asked the team members to describe their reasoning, you would receive a variety of justifications:

- "Multiple stories allow me to multitask! While waiting for code review feedback, I can work on design mockups for another."
- "I'm trying to get ahead on future work."
- "Different items are in different stages, so I'm always busy."

These reasons are absolutely valid, 100 percent. But there could also be unspoken motivations—fear of looking idle, the desire to appear busy, or pressure to show individual progress. These unsaid demands often stem from organizational systems that inadvertently reward "busyness" over outcomes: leadership chasing status updates on multiple initiatives, performance reviews that value productivity numbers over completing valuable work, or cultures that assume visible activity equals effective contribution.

Whatever the case, I've observed that *too much* WIP results in negative impacts to productivity, flow, efficiency, and quality.

Fast forward to day four.

	Day 4		
	Ready	**In Progress**	**Done**
Dusty	Story Story	Story Story Story	
Chase	Story Story	Story Story Story	
Kyle	Story Story	Story Story Story	
Karissa		Story Story Story	
Casey		Story Story Story	
Laurel		Story Story Story	

Interesting, the team's work board appears frozen in time. If it takes three days to complete one story, you'd expect to see several completed stories, right? But instead, you find 18 partially completed stories and zero finished work.

What would six *completed* stories have meant by day four? Working features the PO could validate, demonstrate to stakeholders, and prepare for release—instead of a bunch of half-finished work that can't be tested or validated.

So *why* does the team have 18 partial stories instead of 6 completed ones? **It's because the team members aren't trying to finish one story at a time**, but instead they are juggling multiple stories simultaneously.

And why are they doing that? *Because the organizational culture rewards starting over finishing.* When looking busy matters *more than* completing valuable work, teams will keep spinning up new stories to prove they're industrious—even when that behavior guarantees nothing gets done. This my friends, is known as "productivity theater."

Okay, but if the iteration is two weeks long, the team still has six more business days to complete the work. Why is this a concern at the start of day four?

Valid question. But this isn't just a mathy math problem, it's a "way of thinking problem."

The Illusion of Progress

Let's put ourselves in Dusty's shoes for a moment. He's working on three different stories in parallel:

- Add password reset link to login page.
- Display payment confirmation message.
- Show last login date on user profile.

On day three, each story is in a different state of completion: the password reset has the back-end endpoint but no front-end integration, the payment confirmation has the UI designed but no API connection, and the login date has the database query but no display logic.

This creates several problems:

- **Additional cognitive overhead.** Each time Dusty refocuses on a different story, he has to remember the state of the code, where he left off, and what technical approach he was taking. How do *you* think this context switching impacts his cognitive and mental energy? If you said "not good," you're probably right.
- **Time wasted.** How much time is he spending switching between different codebases? Or remembering which APIs he was integrating? Or rebuilding his mental model of the business logic for each story? This is the time he could have spent actually finishing something.
- **Delayed feedback.** No completed stories = no learning. How long until Dusty receives feedback on working features? What problems might he discover too late? What if he learns that the authentication approach doesn't work with the payment system? How much rework will be needed for the other partially complete stories?

And guess what? Because leaders are *also* juggling multiple initiatives in parallel (sound familiar?), they face identical challenges: mental energy drain from constantly switching between projects and time spent gathering the same information, for different status meetings about a gazillion different projects. Yet somehow, we expect *teams to focus* while leadership models the exact behavior we're trying to avoid?

Clearly, there's wasted time and resources—but the real cost is about how we think about productivity itself. Here's what I've learned: **Starting multiple items *feels* productive, but it's a form of procrastinating on the harder work of finishing.**

True productivity isn't about how many tasks we can juggle—it's about how effectively we can *complete* valuable work. The solution isn't mathematical (better time management) or tactical (better organization)—it requires fundamentally changing *how* we think about and measure progress.

Proof We Suck at Multitasking

What's a delivery change agent to do beyond unsuccessfully attempting to implement WIP limits? (*I know, you've tried.*)

Because this predicament falls mostly unnoticed, the biggest gap is that almost everyone—from team members to leadership—are blind to the indisputable fact that **multitasking is hampering productivity.** There have been numerous studies proving this (along with the decline in product quality) but we all seem to turn a blind eye. Instead, try this easy peasy activity to illuminate this reality:

Whether you're working with your team or facilitating a leadership session, ask participants to grab a piece of paper. Yes, paper. And a writing utensil of sorts. When you say "Go," instruct them to begin their timers, then write **"Multitasking" Is Counterproductive!** exactly as shown down (including the uppercase letters, line breaks, and punctuation). Once complete, ask them to stop their timers and record their time.

Multitasking
Is
Counterproductive!

Direct them to perform this task again, but instead of writing the entire phrase at once, they are to write one letter (or punctuation) per line and to keep repeating this until the entire phrase is written:

"
I
C

Then starting back at the first line …

"M
Is
Co

Then again …

"Mu
Is
Cou

And so on until the entire phrase is complete. They are to start the timer before beginning and then stop it once the phrase has been written completely.

After the group finishes, ask them to share their start and end times. Follow up with probing questions: "What did you notice about the two tasks? How did the first request compare with the second? What surprised you? What would have changed if you had time constraints?" The goal is for them to experience the mental (and possibly emotional) impact multitasking has.

For leadership groups, probe a little more: "How might this apply to managing multiple strategic initiatives? What does this tell us about our current approach to the portfolio?"

This exercise demonstrates how **multitasking dramatically slows us down** rather than making us more efficient. The impact is often most profound on leaders who pride themselves on being great multitaskers. The solution isn't better time management—it's fundamentally changing *how* we think about and measure progress.

The Gift That Costs Nothing

It's not just developers who suffer from context switching—we all do. We, delivery change agents, must face the irrefutable facts about our *own* multitasking addiction. After all, how can we encourage others to focus when we're not practicing it ourselves?

I was facilitating a sprint planning event call with my distributed team, which involved time boxing, engaging the developers, and rerouting the PO when he inevitably took the discussion off course. I was also responding to an e-mail, attempting to craft the perfect response to an urgent matter. On my third monitor, I was fielding rapid fire questions through my chat window. And the cherry on top? I was also figuring out dinner plans via phone text.

I thought I was amazing. *Look at me! I am a multitasking pro! I can do everything, all at once, without even breaking a sweat.*

And then on the call I heard, "Kim, what are your thoughts on this?" Of course, I hadn't been listening so my response was the standard "I'm sorry, can you repeat that?" (which is industry code for "I wasn't listening"). This question rewarded me with an annoyed pause and a sigh before rehashing what had just been discussed.

At that moment, I felt hot embarrassment combined with shame. Here I was, the scrum master for this team, the "servant leader," the *facilitator* of the call, and I wasn't paying attention. I realized I was doing my team an enormous disservice. Not only by neglecting my responsibilities but also by not respecting the framework, the agile mindset, and most importantly, the people.

This was not okay.

And then I realized something else—**my organization was rewarding this *exact* behavior.** In performance reviews, I was praised for being "responsive," for handling multiple priorities simultaneously, for being the person who could "do it all." The culture *rewarded me for being everywhere except where* my job required me to be: present with my team. Crazy, right?

How often are you *truly* present? I'm talking 100 percent engaged? Listening, not just to the words, but for what's between the words. Tuning in for subtle nuances—an uncomfortable giggle, a snort, a pause, a cleansing breath. Noticing the slight shift in energy, a variation of vocal tone, or intonation. How often are you observing? Watching for changes in body language or facial expressions?

When we multitask, we are unconsciously communicating a position of "you're not important enough for my undivided attention." Maybe *you* don't feel this way, but I guarantee that other people do.

Remember this: **presence is a gift that we are either giving or taking away.** Would you rather be a giver or a taker?

You Have Permission to Stay Still

So, here's the million-dollar question: how do we maintain 100 percent presence with this unspoken corporate pressure to get everything done, to answer everything now, and to JUMP WHEN THEY SAY JUMP? Some approaches that may work:

Convey your working style. During casual conversations, be upfront about how you value focus. Let your colleagues know that if you don't respond immediately, it's because you're fully committed to a current task—but you'll follow up by end of day. This helps them understand "You're important to me, I'm just deep in something else right now."

Critical caveat here: Your commitment is only as good as your follow-through. If you fail to get back to them when promised, you will instantly erode the trust you've carefully built. Don't do that.

Strategically manage your messenger status. When leading a conference call or focusing deeply, switch your messenger to "do not disturb." Add an automatic reply: "Hi! I'm not ignoring you but I'm heads down at the moment. I'll respond as soon as I come up for air." This approach respects both your need for concentration and your colleagues' need for acknowledgment.

Close your e-mail. This is the simplest, fastest way to quiet the virtual chatter. Without those persistent pop-up messages, you can stay laser focused on what's happening in the moment. And before you resist—yes, I truly believe you *can* close e-mail. I've never seen the world end, a career implode, or anyone miss something truly urgent by closing e-mail for an hour.

Fiddle with something. A small object can become your anchor to the present moment during calls or meetings. Choose something that helps you stay mindful—perhaps a smooth stone, a small figurine, or a tactile item you can quietly manipulate. By having something to gently spin or move between your hands, you create a subtle physical reminder to stay present and focused.

Lastly, take notes to stay focused. Taking notes—whether in a notebook or on your laptop—creates a powerful tool for active listening. This practice helps you tune in completely to the conversation. If an unrelated thought suddenly surfaces, simply jot it down, and set it aside.

⇧ *Now, Look Up!*

Here's the bottom line: the underlying challenge is *less* about individual multitasking habits and *more* about an organizational culture that rewards and expects constant availability. When companies celebrate people for their "immediate responsiveness" while simultaneously demanding focus, they create an impractical and laughable contradiction. As a delivery change agent, you're positioned to investigate these hidden expectations to create the change you want to see:

Challenge cultural norms. When you're in meetings where engagement seems scattered (long pauses, repeated questions, or obvious distraction), be the one who demonstrates full presence and creates accountability: "I want to make sure we're all aligned on this decision—can everyone confirm they're comfortable with this direction?"

Plant seeds for a better meeting culture. When you're in poorly run meetings, ask questions like "Would it help to limit this conversation to the decision makers?" or "Should we set a time limit to stay focused?" These small suggestions can influence how others run their meetings and may eventually bubble up to leadership as better practices spread throughout the company. Double win!

Help leadership see their role as, well, role models. When you see leaders demonstrating good focus practices, call it out privately: "I saw how engaged everyone was when you put your phone away during that discussion." Or "I noticed how immersed the team became when you reflected back what you heard—it showed you were really listening." This reinforces the behavior without criticizing the opposite.

The harsh reality is that multitasking isn't just about lost productivity—it's about broken connection, missed insights, and diminished impact. When we understand this at a personal level, we're better equipped to help our teams make meaningful changes in how they approach their work.

Crossing the Finish Line

Here's the question of the day: how do you get teams to stop starting and start finishing?

Shine the spotlight on "Done" work. Instead of asking "What are you working on?" which invites discussion about starting and doing—focus your daily check in meetings on completion: "What is preventing this story from moving to done?" or "What is blocking this story from finishing?" or "What's the strategy to wrapping up this work?" This subtle shift in language helps team members think in terms of outcomes rather than just activity, and makes impediments to completion more visible.

Display the iteration burndown and inquire about the next drop. *I see we're flatlining here, which story is closest to being done? Let's breathe some life back into this sprint!* This strategy shifts focus from all the in-progress work to what's nearly complete, encouraging the team to push something across the finish line rather than letting everything remain partially done.

Celebrate completions, not starts. Instead of acknowledging when someone picks up work, celebrate when the work is complete. By "celebrate," I mean engage in merriment: make a big deal out of it! Pop on a silly party hat, bang a gong, or play an upbeat song. This subtle shift reinforces completion as the valuable outcome.

⇧ *Now, Look Up!*

These completion-focused strategies work just as well with leadership teams who struggle to finalize decisions, projects, and commitments before starting new ones. Consider how you might adapt these approaches within the system:

Shine the spotlight on unresolved decisions. In leadership meetings, shift from "What are we discussing today?" to "What decisions from last week still require closure?" or "What's preventing us from finalizing <fill in the blank>?" This change in focus encourages leaders to *finish* incomplete work *before* starting new discussions, just like you want teams to finish stories before starting new ones. Essentially, you're encouraging leadership to drink from their own champagne glass.

Celebrate closed decisions and completed commitments, not just new discussions. Leader's love *starting* new strategic conversations but rarely acknowledge when they *finish* what they started. Try calling out completed work in real time: "We finally closed the vendor decision today—the one that's been open for three weeks. This is fantastic progress!" This simple recognition reinforces completion as an admirable behavior.

These strategies can help both teams and leadership focus on finishing work. But even with the best completion practices in place, a bigger challenge remains—the constant stream of requests competing for attention.

When Everything Is High Priority

As teams begin to recognize the true cost of juggling multiple items, they often discover a deeper issue: the stream of new work keeps coming because nobody wants to say "no." Remember that design request? That's just one example of how saying "yes" to everything creates exactly the kind of chaos we just explored.

When Danielle (the CTO) approached Kyle (the developer) about tightening up the UI before the next board meeting, it wasn't just about new unplanned work—it was about prioritization. Kyle faced a common dilemma: keep his commitment to the team's sprint goal or bow to a senior leader's request. This kind of situation forces team members to make difficult choices between competing priorities, *often without the tools or support to make those decisions effectively.*

And let's be perfectly real here—saying no to a senior leader feels dangerous and risky. Team members often worry about being labeled "uncooperative" or "inflexible," fearing that this could impact their career growth (or quite frankly, their job).

Unfortunately, these fears *aren't* unfounded—organizations often select people for being "flexible" and "team players," and then those same people struggle to say no to unrealistic requests. And there's usually social pressure too—do **you** want to be the one saying "no" to the CTO? *I didn't think so.*

Here's the thing about prioritization: It's not about saying no—it's about making informed decisions.

When new requests arrive, our goal isn't to turn them down, but to make them visible so that we can consciously decide what to do with them. *The real challenge aren't the requests themselves, but the lack of a clear process for handling them.*

The Impossible Choice

When faced with competing demands, we often try to promise both: "Sure, I'll redesign the UI ***and*** finish my sprint stories!" But this isn't a realistic solution—Kyle has to choose.

Either he works on the UI **or** he works on reducing patient setup time. Pretending that he can do everything just leads to missed commitments, rushed work, and high blood pressure. The real challenge is making an informed choice about what takes priority. Simple, right?

I have only one brain.	If I say yes to this feature.	Then I say yes to UI changes.	I've now said no to the feature.	Because I can't do both simultaneously.
				or

And when it comes to future work, I've experienced this type of conversation so many times in my career that I can practically recite it from memory. It usually goes like this:

Me (looking at a list of 40 upcoming epics): "What's the highest priority item?"

PO: "They all are!"

Me: "Yes, but which ***must*** be done first?"

PO (with increasing intensity): "They **all** need to be done first!"

Often, POs are squawking back the *exact same directive* they are hearing from leadership: "We have to complete the market expansion, the platform upgrade, *and* the customer retention initiative, all within this quarter!" This is a pattern that cascades from the strategic level down to the team level.

And the exchange would be oh so funny if it weren't so painfully familiar. The problem with this is very straightforward: **If everything is the highest priority, nothing is.** Thus, adding to the significant waste in the system. Look, trying to do everything at once creates waste in several ways:

It wastes time. Endless meetings with leadership and stakeholders reprioritizing the "top priorities" *every single time* someone changes their mind. This results in teams bouncing like ping pong balls between work based on whoever shouted loudest that day, rebuilding context at every switch. Talk about whiplash!

It lowers morale. Teams burn out trying to do it all, their efforts spread peanut butter style, across multiple projects. Frustration builds as people feel powerless to influence the constant chaos.

Opportunities are lost. Truly important work gets delayed and market opportunities are lost due to indecisiveness and Fear of Making a Wrong Decision (FOMAWD). Always remember: **not making a decision *is* making a decision.**

Quality suffers. When our attention is divided, we've overcommitted, and time is running out, quality is the first thing that suffers. Think about the last time you dropped your keys, stubbed your toe, or spilled your water bottle due to rushing around like a frantic squirrel late for an acorn convention.

When everything is the "highest priority," effectively nothing is priority—leading to inefficient use of team capacity and accumulated waste *across the entire organization*. This pattern doesn't *just* affect teams—it impacts leadership decisions, strategic initiatives, and people allocation at every level. But there are ways you can support your PO and team, and influence the broader organizational culture around prioritization.

Breaking Through Paralysis

Communicating clear priorities is one of the PO's primary jobs. And it's *brutal*—they're juggling business value, customer needs, technical feasibility, people, timelines, and risk all at once. Having done this myself, I can tell you this is not a frivolous or straightforward task. Truth is, it's the exact opposite: it's like trying to juggle flaming torches while riding a unicycle—you need to keep multiple items in the air, maintain your balance, and somehow make it all look smooth and deliberate.

Are you ready to help your PO shatter this "everything is urgent" cycle, once and for all? I know I am.

Start by familiarizing yourself with prioritization strategies such as MoSCoW or Value versus Effort so that you can **guide a prioritization workshop** with your PO and stakeholders. By directing the conversation using formal approaches, you are creating a decision-making process that is more objective and less emotional.

When you hear executives struggling with competing strategic priorities, suggest facilitating a similar workshop with the leadership team. Frame it as helping them model solid prioritization practices for the organization: "What if we used this same framework to align on our top three strategic initiatives?" Often, leaders who are shaping the "everything is urgent" culture haven't experienced structured prioritization themselves.

Then, help your PO and stakeholders articulate their underlying needs rather than dictate the solutions. Here's a common example of this: A stakeholder contacts the PO "We need a weekly PDF report showing all customer support tickets, their status, and response times. This needs to be done yesterday!"

Instead of immediately prioritizing the report, you can **help guide a deeper dialog by getting curious and asking questions that get to the root of the why**: *What decisions would this report help you make? What would having this data help you achieve? How would you use this information to make improvements?*

These answers may reveal alternative solutions that solve the problem more effectively, quickly or easily, which transforms the prioritization process from a feature wish-list into strategic value delivery.

⇧ *Now, Look Up!*

Beyond facilitating workshops, there are other ways to influence the organizational source of priority dysfunction:

Suggest a visual project board for leadership. When you see leaders mentally juggling all those competing projects, propose creating a visual board similar to what teams use: "What if we created a project board showing your current quarterly projects and programs?" This makes overcommitment obvious without directly confronting their tendency to take on too much. When they see 12 projects in "In Progress," the problem becomes self-evident and they will often start regulating their own workload.

Recommend simple priority change processes. When you witness teams getting blindsided by constant priority shifts, propose introducing lightweight checks: "What if we had a lightweight process for when new priorities come up—like asking 'what stops if we start this?' or having priority changes go through the same people who approved the original priorities?"

Framing this from a *team protection perspective*, rather than a "you suck, stop doing this to your people" perspective helps leadership see the impacts of sudden priority changes. They are more likely to engage when the sentiment is "let's help teams prepare" and not "please stop creating chaos."

Transform "shiny new object" energy into finishing momentum. When leaders get energized about starting something new, help redirect that energy toward finishing existing work first: "Great idea! What would need to be completed first to free up the team for this?" The key is *channeling their enthusiasm* rather than dampening it—you're not saying no to the new idea, you're helping them sequence it strategically.

Let's be honest—changing how an organization thinks about and handles priorities is far from easy. It requires patience, persistence, and a willingness to have uncomfortable conversations. But the alternative—continuing to pretend everything *can* be the highest priority—costs far more in the long run.

Connect the Dots and Take Action

When organizations feel pressure to reduce costs, they often reach for the visible solution: slashing headcount. But as we've seen throughout this chapter, the most significant drains on productivity and profit are often invisible—hidden in unplanned requests, WIP overload, and the inability to prioritize effectively. What we've discussed:

- **Unplanned work has a massive context switching tax.** This includes time spent rebuilding mental models, recovering momentum, and fixing rushed work. But here's what most people miss: the problem isn't individual team members saying "yes" —it's organizational dysfunction. When no one knows who has authority, priorities compete for attention, and "emergency" means nothing, unplanned work becomes inevitable.
- **Too much WIP kills productivity at every single level.** Starting multiple items *feels* productive, but it's procrastinating on the harder work of finishing. We (teams and leaders) all fall into this trap.
- **When everything is a high priority, nothing is.** When leadership can't choose between competing projects, teams inherit impossible prioritization problems. The dysfunction flows from the strategic level all the way down to the team level.

Kyle's story showed us the real cost of saying yes to everything—not just the 12 hours spent on the application design, but the context switching recovery time, the quality issues from rushed work, and the team commitment that got derailed. The multitasking exercise proved what research already knows—we're terrible at juggling multiple tasks simultaneously.

The solution isn't working harder—*it's finishing work before starting new work*, protecting focus time, and creating organizational conditions that support concentration over busyness.

You're uniquely positioned to address these productivity drains at both levels: At the team level by helping teams protect their flow, complete their work, and handle unplanned requests strategically. And at the systems level by influencing leadership to model better focus, establish clear boundaries, and make informed decisions about priorities.

Here's my challenge for you

Before diving into large-scale changes, start by making the invisible visible by tracking the impact of unplanned interruptions over the course of a few sprints.

The Costs of Unplanned Work

Frequency and Source of the Unplanned Work

- ❑ Number of unplanned requests per iteration
- ❑ The requestor's name
- ❑ Request type (urgent fixes, new enhancements, research etc.)

Time Impact

- ❑ Context switching recovery time
- ❑ Actual time spent on the unplanned work
- ❑ Time lost on the original planned work

Iteration Impact

- ❑ Number of planned stories that didn't get completed
- ❑ Percentage of team capacity consumed by unplanned work
- ❑ Number of items carried over to next iteration (roll over)

This data can tell you:

- Which types of interruptions are most costly.
- Whether certain team members get interrupted more than others.
- The impact on team commitments.
- Patterns in when/where interruptions occur.
- The real cost of "quick requests."

But don't stop with just tracking unplanned work. Pick one additional technique from this chapter:

- Run the multitasking exercise with your team or leadership to prove the cost of context switching.
- Experiment with the "one in, one out" rule when urgent requests arrive.
- Help your team establish focus time signals and boundaries.
- Guide a prioritization workshop using MoSCoW or Value versus Effort techniques.

When you can show that a team spending 20 percent of their time on unplanned work delivers 40 percent less value, you've got *powerful data* to drive change at all levels. Here are a few reflection questions as you move forward:

- Which organizational patterns are you noticing repeatedly in your organization?
- Where do you have the most influence to create change—with teams or leadership?
- What would success look like if your organization truly embraced focus over busyness?
- How might you start conversations about these systemic issues without putting people on the defensive?

Remember: The goal isn't to eliminate all interruptions or urgent requests—it's to make them visible so we can make informed decisions about their true necessity and cost.

Once you start tracking and reducing these productivity drains, you often discover yet *another* layer of waste that's been quietly hiding underneath what you've already uncovered—knowledge silos, specialist bottlenecks, and the "that's not my job" mentality that keeps teams dependent, fragile, and oh so slow.

CHAPTER 6

Competitive Disadvantage—We're Getting Crushed by Start-Ups Half Our Size

You've started tracking all those productivity drains—the context switching, the multitasking madness, and the constant interruptions. You're making the invisible visible, just like we discussed. But sadly, once you peel back that first layer, you're going to find something *even more* frustrating lurking underneath. And it's probably why your company is at a disadvantage.

Your team is developing "Bread2Toast (B2T)," a mobile application set to modernize breakfast communications by sending real-time text updates on a bread's journey from pallor to toastiness. B2T is poised to disrupt breakfast anxiety by eliminating the uncertainty around bread's most pivotal browning moment, finally freeing consumers from their angsty toaster hovering (*admit it, you hover*).

Although customers are clamoring for the app, the product is several quarters behind schedule, putting your team under a scorching spotlight. You've been asked to investigate why this revolutionary bread-tracking technology still remains half-baked. The directive is clear: "We need to understand why we are so far behind schedule or we're toast!" (*Oh, the puns don't stop coming, do they?*)

But here's what you know that others might miss: when start-ups half your size are moving faster, it's rarely about individual team performance. It's usually about organizational inefficiencies that's invisible to leadership, but crystal clear to people like you who see the whole system.

You shift into investigative mode, determined to uncover the systemic issues impacting productivity. Like a seasoned detective, you focus on one critical question: *Where is the waste?* And this question is being posed at two levels:

- What's slowing down your *team's* daily work?
- What *organizational patterns* are creating these constraints in the first place?

Silent Sneaky Waste

What exactly *is* "waste?" And how do we recognize it?

My friend Arien, an insightful and articulate scrum master, simply explains that waste is "needless extra." Dictionary.com defines this as: '*Useless consumption or expenditure; use without adequate return; an act or instance of wasting.*'

When considering software development, what can be "wasted?" (*Insert excessive alcohol consumption joke here.*) You already know the classics: money, time, energy, and material. But what about those undercover ones: opportunity, talent, knowledge, innovation, trust, motivation? Or … focus, momentum, creativity, expertise, goodwill, market advantage, morale, or cognitive abilities? There's a feast of wastefulness around every single corner! It's one of the critical reasons why we aren't moving as quickly as we would like to.

You're uniquely positioned to spot these hidden disruptions because you see what others don't. While leadership focuses on visible costs like salaries and tools, you witness the invisible drains: the constant context switching that rattles your team's focus, the knowledge silos that create bottlenecks, and the organizational norms that force teams to work *around* dysfunction rather than through it.

Start-ups move faster not because they have more talented people, but because they haven't accumulated the organizational crap that slows down larger companies. (Not yet, anyway.) You can effectively help your company discover and eliminate these productivity killers before they become "the way it's always been."

The Underdog That Changed Everything

Quick history lesson: In post-WWII Japan, Toyota Automobile engineers Taiichi Ohno and Shigeo Shingo faced a wall of challenges: very little money, lack of material, and a restricted labor market. Unlike American manufacturers who could rely on mass production and abundant resources, Toyota needed a different approach to survive. "Lean manufacturing"—a method that focused more on customer value and less on waste—was born.

At its heart was a straightforward concept: identify and eliminate anything that doesn't add customer value (like idle time waiting, energy in motion, or unused inventory). This simple, innovative approach *transformed* Toyota from an industry underdog into an industry leader.

What I find fascinating is that the same principle applies to organizational systems—and life, really, when you think about it.

Just as Toyota identified inefficiencies in manufacturing, you can spot the same systemic problems in how work flows through your organization. The only difference is that manufacturing issues are often visible on the factory floor, while organizational friction hides in meetings, handoffs, approval processes, and cultural patterns that everyone just accepts as "this is how we do things here." (Insert long, deep sigh)

Let's take this out of the office environment and into everyday life. For a moment, reflect on a typical trip to your local grocery store or market. Consider the store layout, the selections available to choose from, and the checkout process. Try to visualize your experience through the lens of "needless, extra." What do *you* see as unnecessary?

Maybe you notice the extra packaging—*why is that bag of potato chips only one-third full when opened?* Or maybe it's the surplus of vegetables you must buy—*why am I forced to purchase a three-pound bag of carrots when the recipe calls for just* ***one*** *carrot*? Or maybe the peanut butter is five aisles away from the jars of jam, or that the bakery "sale rack" is overflowing with loaves of stale sourdough bread? Where else do you spot the waste?

The Only Waste Checklist You Need

Those everyday examples illustrate how inefficiency surrounds us, often unnoticed until we deliberately search for it. The same is true in your organization—this "needless extra" becomes so normalized that people *stop* seeing it.

Lean practitioners originally identified eight specific types of manufacturing waste, now remembered through the acronym "DOWNTIME" (or if you're feeling saucy: "TIMED NOW"). Software professionals adopted this same observational approach and discovered that these translate perfectly to software development (as illustrated in the following diagram).

	Waste	Questions to help you find it
D	Defects	What gets rewarded - hitting deadlines or fixing things right?
O	Overproduction	Do we build features nobody requested because we're afraid to say no?
W	Waiting	When decisions are needed, does anyone know who *actually* decides?
N	Non-Utilized Talent	Are smart people told what to build instead being given problems to solve?
T	Transportation	Does every department insist on their own special tools?
I	Inventory	Do we start new things before finishing what we already started?
M	Motion	Do we avoid automating because "we don't have the time" to save time?
E	Extra Processing	Are we afraid to ship anything less than perfect?

Chart defining eight types of organizational waste with icons and diagnostic questions for identifying each type.

- **Defects:** This inefficiency is pretty obvious. It refers to errors or mistakes requiring rework such as bugs or hotfixes following a production release. Defects are expensive—they trigger a cascade of additional documentation, testing, debugging, development, and validation work that wasn't originally planned for. And that's just the internal cost!

  When defects find their way to customers, they damage your company's reputation and erode trust that's *ridiculously* hard to rebuild. The worst part is that most defects could have been prevented with better practices earlier in the process, which is why "shifting left" has become such a crucial concept in modern development.

Shift Left	What does it mean to "*shift left?*" Rather than just pulling testing activities to the front of the timeline, it's about integrating a "whole team quality" mindset *from the very beginning*. This means baking quality into every step—discussing test strategy during story discussions, creating test tasks at planning, and brainstorming how to approach quality during development. By embedding this type of thinking at the start, we're *preventing* defects rather than discovering them.

Systems View: When you see persistent defect patterns, look up—what organizational pressures are creating them? Unrealistic deadlines? Competing priorities? Performance metrics that reward speed over stability? The defects aren't always a team problem; more often they're symptoms of systemic dysfunction.

- **Overproduction:** Overproduction is creating more than what's needed or creating something *before* it's needed, leading to excess inventory. In software development, this correlates to building features that users haven't requested or creating reports no one will use. It's like writing extra code that no one has asked for yet.

  The easiest way to identify possible overproduction ahead of time, is to ask: "Does this feature directly contribute to customer value?" Said another way: Is this a "nice to have" or a "must have?" If it's a nice to have, then let's pause and focus our energy instead on what is required first.

  From a systems perspective: When teams continually build features nobody asked for, look up—what's driving this behavior? Is it unclear strategy? Fear of saying no? Or maybe your culture rewards "being busy bees" over value delivery? The true inefficiency aren't the extra features created, it's the organization's inability to prioritize (*and* stick with those priorities).
- **Waiting:** Idle time when work stops because the next process step isn't ready. This could be a stalled communication, a peer review in limbo, a decision that never comes, an approval stuck

in someone's inbox, or simply an acknowledgment that takes forever. This sounds innocent enough—"we're just waiting to hear back from the business"—but it creates massive cascading process delays that crush overall productivity.

From a systems perspective: When teams are constantly waiting for approvals, decisions, or feedback, look up—what organizational bottlenecks are creating these delays? Who's the one who makes the decisions? Is there an excessive amount of approval steps? Perhaps leaders are overwhelmed and juggling too many things? These delays aren't just about lost productivity; they're also a symptom of broken (or nonexistent) processes.

- **Non-utilized Talent:** Have you ever felt undervalued in your role? As if your talents are completely being overlooked? This happens when we underuse people's knowledge, skills, abilities, or talents. For example, when teams are simply handed solutions to implement (rather than problems to solve), they're forced directly into execution mode, wasting their creativity, curiosity, and subject–matter expertise.

  This waste extends *far beyond* lost productivity—it weakens engagement and silences innovation. When organizations ignore what their people are capable of, they get exactly what they deserve: demotivated employees, zero ingenuity, and eventually, carefully crafted resignation letters.

  From a systems perspective: When talented people are relegated to "order takers," look up—what's really driving this? Command and control leaders who don't trust the people doing the work? Managers who think they know better than the experts they hired? Cultures where asking questions is seen as anarchy or disrespect? The waste isn't just lost productivity; it's lost innovation and eventually, broken people.

- **Transportation:** Transportation refers to unnecessary movement of materials or information. In the world of software development, this waste is the needless shuffling of data, code, or information between systems or teams.

  Think about someone building a product roadmap in PowerPoint, completely ignoring the existing roadmap in your organization's planning platform. This perfectly illustrates transportation waste because the information is being unnecessarily "transported" from a purpose-built system to a presentation tool, creating redundancy and extra work. (I can hear you now: "What a waste!!" Yes, I agree!)

From a systems perspective: When information gets unnecessarily shuffled between systems, look up—what's forcing this redundancy? Departments that refuse to talk to each other? Overlapping tools that enable political turf wars? Teams that hoard information like toilet paper during COVID? The redundant work is bad enough, but the silos creating it are the *real* problem.

- **Inventory:** Inventory relates to excess products or materials waiting to be processed. This can be tricky to grasp in software development since we don't have tangible things sitting on shelves. But we absolutely have inventory waste!

  Consider all those stories that were refined last quarter but keep getting deprioritized month after month, their requirements growing stale. Or the partially completed stories that roll over between iterations, neither done nor delivering value. You might also have code that's been written, but not deployed, or features that are "almost ready" but remain in that state for weeks. All of that in-progress work that's not delivering value is pure inventory waste.

  From a systems perspective: When work piles up without delivering value, look up—what's creating this? Competing priorities that prevent anything from finishing? Unclear definitions of what "done" really means? Cultures that reward starting new things over completing old ones? The inventory isn't just delayed value; it's evidence of systemic focus problems.
- **Motion:** In lean manufacturing, motion refers to unnecessary movement of people—it's the equivalent of grabbing a jar of peanut butter and then traveling five more aisles for the low sugar strawberry jam. But in software development, this isn't about physical movement. Motion waste shows up when we're doing repetitive manual tasks that beg to be automated—like manually running the same tests over and over, copying and pasting code between files, or going through a 15-step deployment process that could be reduced to a single click.

It's all that extra clicking, typing, and mental context-switching that keeps us busy without adding value. These tiny inefficiencies might seem minor in isolation, but they drain our energy and focus.

From a systems perspective: When teams spend time on repetitive manual tasks, look up—what's preventing automation? Organizations that would rather save a dollar today than save a hundred tomorrow? Skill gaps that nobody wants to address? Cultures that see manual work as being "meticulous or careful?" The clicks and keystrokes aren't just wasted time; they're symptoms of short-sightedness.

- **Excess Processing:** This is where we are doing more work than required to meet customer needs, also known as "gold plating." You may have heard this term—it means to create overly complex architectures for simple problems or to write extensive documentation that no one will *ever* read.

  It's that developer who adds elaborate error handling for that "one in a million" edge case instead of focusing on the common failure scenarios. Or the tester who spends days creating detailed bug reports with screenshots, videos, and step-by-step instructions for minor UI inconsistencies that don't impact user experience.

  We think we're adding value, but we're primarily just adding complexity without benefit. Our intentions are always good—we want to do our best work—but we need to constantly assess whether this additional effort will matter to our customers (or not).

  From a systems perspective: When teams overengineer solutions, look up—what fears are driving this perfectionism? Cultures that punish any failure? Unclear requirements that force teams to guess at what's needed? Performance reviews that reward complexity over simplicity? Gold plating isn't just wasted effort; it's a defense mechanism against some sort of organizational dysfunction.

Whether it's in the number of bugs being introduced, the incessant context switching, excessive WIP, or a culture of perfection over progress, these inefficiencies are literally everywhere.

The Barnacles Sinking Your Ship

Okay, so why should you care? Because all this needless extra slows us down. **It's like barnacles on a cruise ship—each tiny inefficiency creates drag, gradually slowing your progress until you're barely moving.** This is one of the primary reasons we aren't getting to market sooner.

Up to this point, we've tackled a number of wasteful practices such as:

- Accommodating for unplanned work.
- Excessive context switching.
- Countless production support issues.
- Circular discussions.
- Too much WIP.
- Multitasking.
- Focusing on outputs rather than outcomes.
- Lack of prioritization.
- Overwhelming technical debt.

Now, let's apply this waste detection lens back to our B2T scenario from this chapter's introduction. When you investigate why this app remains behind schedule, your trained eye quickly identifies various forms of time sinks hiding in plain sight. After careful observation and some targeted conversations, you uncover several issues that align perfectly with the DOWNTIME categories we just explored:

Bread2Toast Observations	Primary Waste
The tester sits idle while developers are working, then becomes overwhelmed at sprint's end	*Waiting*
Distinct knowledge silos exist where only specific individuals can work on certain parts of the codebase	*Non-Utilized Talent*
Work is sitting in various stages of completion instead of being brought to "done"	*Inventory*
"We've always done it this way" mentality is preventing optimization	*Motion*
Developers are overengineering solutions in isolation	*Extra Processing*

Clearly, there are numerous areas where time, energy, and momentum are being wasted. Considered separately, each might seem manageable, but combined? It's death by a thousand papercuts! These aren't just minor inconveniences either—they're the untold story behind why this toast tracking technology remains stuck. Here's your chance to shine by exposing (and addressing) these hidden productivity killers.

Susie Can't take Vacation

During an earlier coaching engagement, like déjà vu, the name "Susie" kept popping up again and again in various meetings ("Susie will know about this." or "Check with Susie on that.") Susie had been with the company for 27 years and had coded their core platform. With that longevity came *tremendous* tribal knowledge.

When I met Susie over coffee, she mentioned her 220 hours of unused personal time off (PTO) because she "could not be unavailable for more than a few hours at a time." This is a classic sign of having one single point of failure (SPOF).

What if Susie won the mega millions jackpot tomorrow? Would she still badge into the office for that 8:00 a.m. status meeting or greet her colleagues with a cheery "Happy funday Monday!" in team chat? Probably not. And the company would be scrambling to fill an impossible knowledge gap.

But here's what you need to understand: Susie didn't become an SPOF overnight. These dependencies develop organically as organizations naturally turn to their most knowledgeable people again and again. So, how do you spot an SPOF? The warning signs are usually clear:

- They're constantly in demand, with statements like "We can't start until Susie arrives."
- They hold exclusive access to systems or information others need.
- There's often a "hero" mentality, where they are the first to dive into that burning dumpster fire.
- Others happily step back, thinking "better her than me!"

But SPOFs aren't the only way specialists create bottlenecks. There's another pattern that's just as damaging: the "that's not my job" mentality.

Have you ever witnessed a team member decline work that needed to be done because it simply wasn't "what they do?" While specialization might *seem* efficient on the surface, this type of rigid role definition creates bottlenecks, reduces flexibility, irritates other team members, and ultimately drives up costs.

When team members can only perform one type of task, work doesn't flow—it starts and stops based on who's available.

We talk a good game about "cross-functional teams," but what are we actually saying? The phrase "cross-functional" refers to a team that possesses a diverse set of skills necessary to complete all aspects of the project. But here's an important distinction—you can have a cross-functional team without cross-functional individuals. Your team might have a specialized tester, specialized front-end developer, and specialized back-end developer, making it *technically* "cross-functional" as a unit. But this arrangement is brittle—what happens when your only tester is sick or overwhelmed?

Software development is a *team* sport—we're playing basketball here, not tennis. Like a basketball player who needs to both defend and score, team members need to be versatile.

I've found that a fixed "my job is to X" mindset is a major contributor in delivery inefficiencies (and increased costs). The problem with this mentality is that team members are only thinking in terms of "me, mine" and not "we, ours."

Said another way, the goal isn't to complete "my stories," or to complete "the tasks that I specialize in," **the primary objective is for "the team" to complete the most valuable work**; which means sometimes focusing on tasks that may not be exclusive to their role. You hear this mindset in the words being used, or in the way work is allocated even before the sprint begins ("Karissa will take that story since she's done this before, Chase will work on that one," etc.)

This individual ownership mentality runs deeper than you might think. While coaching a team on swarming, I encountered *major* resistance from developers who kept pushing back on shared story ownership. This confused me because … to put it bluntly, *who cares*? After a candid conversation, I uncovered the real issue: developers feared that without their individual names on stories, management would think that they weren't doing any work. (Later this was debunked, but the fear was very real.)

⇧ *Now, Look Up!*

Understanding the underlying system that creates specialist bottlenecks is just as important as identifying them. This story reveals a classic organizational dysfunction: systems that *claim* to embrace teamwork but reward individual heroics. When you encounter this type of resistance, ask yourself:

- What organizational patterns are encouraging this behavior?
- Is individual productivity recognized over team outcomes?
- Do performance reviews reward expertise over collaboration?
- Does the culture reward quick action over knowledge sharing?
- Is the organization specifically hiring specialists instead of versatile contributors?
- What is preventing cross-training? Budget constraints, maybe?
- Are upward mobility career paths available only for those with narrow skillsets?
- Are "expensive" people protected from doing menial or lower skilled work?

This creates the "that's not my job" culture we talked about earlier, where expertise becomes a weapon instead of a tool. People hoard knowledge to stay valuable, creating SPOFs that bottleneck every project they touch.

From Work Hoarders to Team Players

How can you address these dysfunctions? Assuming that your influence is limited:

- **Identify the vulnerabilities** by asking: "What would come to a screeching halt if the SPOF quit tomorrow?" What would make others blurt "shit!" when hearing the news?

- **Make these risks visible to leadership** and the team.
- **Document the cost of silos.** Track delays caused by waiting for specific people and present the consequences. Keep a simple log of incidents like "Feature was delayed three days waiting for Rachel to review database changes" or "Testing was blocked for two days until Shawn returned from vacation."
- **Create and socialize a strategic plan** for knowledge sharing through pair programming, documentation, and cross-training.
- **Recommend adding specific backlog items** focused on distributing knowledge to the team's work board.
- **Make team outcomes visible to leadership.** Create dashboards or reports that focus on *team* velocity and completion rates rather than individual stories.

And if you have broader influence:

- **Restructure teams** to include members with overlapping skills rather than one specialist per function.
- **Adjust the hiring criteria** to lean more on learning ability and collaboration over narrow expertise.
- **Expand administrative access** to critical systems to *at least* two people.
- **Allocate dedicated learning time** for cross training and knowledge sharing.
- **Incorporate collaboration in the performance review criteria.** Add expectations like "helps teammates succeed" or "shares knowledge freely" right next to "delivers high quality code." Make *teamwork* count for raises and promotions, not *individual heroics.*
- **Track and communicate** the real cost of knowledge silos when key people are unavailable. Put a bright red price tag on it—calculate the overtime costs, project delays, and stress-related turnover.
- **Change what you celebrate.** For the love of God, please stop giving shout outs to the *person* who saved the day. Instead, *celebrate the team that prevented the crisis* by working together. **Keep in mind, what gets publicly recognized gets repeated.**

The goal isn't just to fix today's knowledge bottlenecks—it is to design or influence the organizational patterns that *prevent* them from forming tomorrow.

The Shape That Saves Teams

You may have also heard the term "T-shaped skills" (or "specializing generalists"), which means having both breadth and depth of expertise. It's about fusing specialized knowledge with a general understanding of other proficiencies to enhance teamwork and problem-solving.

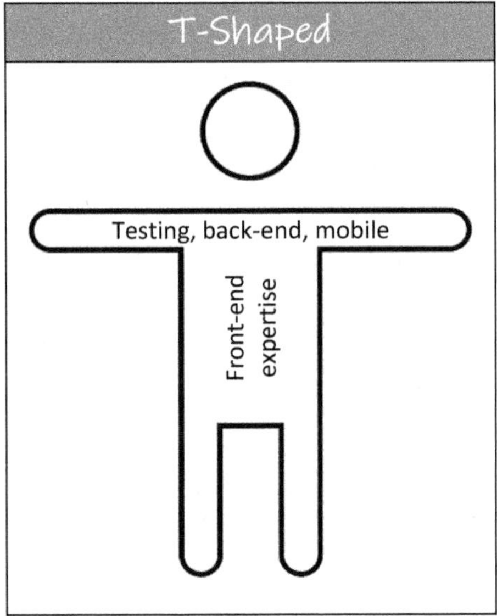

For example, as an engineer on her team, Becca has deep knowledge in front-end development (since that is her functional area or discipline), but she can work outside this area helping the team with manual testing, back-end work, and mobile app development. She may not produce mind-blowing outputs, but she's sufficient and can support the workload when needed. Becca would be considered "T-shaped."

Why does this matter? T-shaped team members solve the specialist bottleneck problems we just explored. Because Becca can step in to help with testing, the team doesn't get stuck waiting for that one tester. When she can review back-end code, knowledge isn't trapped with a single developer. T-shaped skills build the resilience and flexibility that specialist teams simply cannot match.

You may be wondering—how exactly do you build these capabilities? A few of my favorite methods include:

- **Scheduled lunch and learns.** The title says it all: arrive with your deli sandwich and an appetite for learning. One person takes the role as a trainer, teaching the participants new techniques, skills, or applications that are pertinent to the work the team is (or will be) doing. This allows team members to cross pollinate and integrate real-life scenarios applicable to their current or future workload.

  Lunch and learns aren't just for in-office training—even if the team is remote, they can jump on a zoom call and participate as normal. Make sure to rotate the topic and the speaker so that everyone gets a chance to lead.
- **Taking advantage of learning days.** *Wait, what? I see the word "day" and as we know that could be eight+ hours. No one has time for a whole day of learning! We have real work to do!*

  Would it surprise you to learn that Fidelity Investments, a Fortune 500 company specializing in financial services and investment products, has implemented *one entire day* out of every week, dedicated to associate development? That's 52 Tuesdays in a year if you're counting, where they set aside one undivided day for learning. During this time, employees are *expected* to innovate, study, explore, and absorb new skills to help them progress in their career. How cool is that? What would it take for your company to implement learning days?
- **Double down with pair programming.** This is where two programmers team up to work alongside one another. One of the two programmers (the driver) writes the code, while the other watches and reviews (the observer). This is an excellent training method because the quality of the code is higher (two minds are better than one) and developers are learning together.

You don't need to become the training coordinator, but you can advocate for and help organize these learning opportunities when you spot skill gaps that are slowing down delivery.

⇧ *Now, Look Up!*

So, let's say you've proposed these learning approaches and are told "we don't have time for that." What organization dysfunction might you be seeing?

- Managers who can't connect the dots between cross-training time and fewer bottlenecks?
- A culture that doesn't view learning as "real work?"
- A company that is so busy fighting fires they never have time to install sprinklers?
- Managers who protect their specialists because they think cross-training dilutes expertise?

How you respond to these dysfunctions depends of course, on your level of influence. If your influence is limited:

- **Advocate for knowledge-sharing performance incentives**, and not just individual achievements. What if collaboration was visibly measured and rewarded, not just expected?
- **Challenge the hero culture** when the hero is being praised for their hero-ness. Try redirecting the dialog: "Susie is indeed awesome. I'm wondering though, what can we try in the future to eliminate this overreliance on one person?"
- **Weave in cross-training** (organically). Don't make a big deal out of it. Simply encourage developers to pair program or share knowledge during quiet moments, without making it into this big formal thing requiring approval and bureaucracy.
- **Devote informal time for knowledge sharing.** Start a 15-minute "coffee and code" session before your regular team meetings, or suggest people hop on a casual call to walk through something they're working on. No formal agenda, just friendly sharing.

- **Raise this during the team's retrospectives.** Don't sweep these dysfunctions under the rug! When delays happen due to specialist bottlenecks, bring them up during the team retrospectives. You want the team to acknowledge the negative impact the team faced so that *they* can identify viable solutions.
- **Have a heart to heart with the SPOF.** Point out that being irreplaceable often means being stuck—they can't take uninterrupted vacation days, can't move to other projects, and can't grow beyond their current role because the organization depends on them too much. I mean, who wants that?
- **Do the same with the managers**. Help them understand that tracking individual productivity is like measuring how many passes each player completes instead of looking at whether the team wins games. *Team results matter more than individual metrics.*
- **Celebrate collaborative wins.** When team members work together to complete stories faster and with higher quality, communicate this awesomeness. For example: "This week, when our front-end developer helped with testing, we caught three bugs before they reached production and delivered this work two days ahead of schedule."

If you have broader influence:

- **Explain the impact of "specialist protection."** Talk with leadership: "When our Java developer was out sick for three days, our top priorities just sat there waiting." Cross-training isn't intended to dilute expertise—it's about making sure that one person calling in sick doesn't ruin the plan.
- **Challenge the "expensive people shouldn't do cheap work" mindset.** This thinking usually stems from real budget pressures—when you're paying developers significantly more than testers, it feels logical to keep them focused on "developer work." But help leaders see that a pricey developer who can test

is infinitely more valuable than one who creates bottlenecks by only doing specialized work. Suggest hiring "quality engineers" who can both code *and* test to change the dynamic.

- **Confront management's fears head on.** Many managers worry that their amazing Java expert will hate the other tasks they are being asked to do and quit. I mean, yeah, that's a valid concern. And obviously, we don't want to force anyone into work they hate. Instead, suggest that managers ask their people what they *want* to learn (what a novel concept!). Maybe the developer *wants* to learn DevOps, or the tester *wants* to try automation. Suggest that the manager work *with* their interests, not against them.
- **Address the salary disparity that reinforces the expensive versus cheap work bias mentioned previously.** When testers earn significantly less than developers, it's easy to see testing as "lower value work." Consider leveling compensation for team members with complementary skills.
- **Change the employee's performance review criteria.** Include T-shaped skill development as a measurable goal. Reward people for learning new skills and teaching others, not just for staying in their lane.
- (*Or even better*) **Change how managers are evaluated.** Make developing T-shaped team members part of the manager's performance reviews. If their own career advancement depends on building versatile employees, suddenly cross-training becomes the newest, shiniest thing.
- **Implement mandatory cross-training opportunities:** Build skill development into every iteration, track who's learning what. As an incentive, tie learning and teaching to bonuses, promotions, or team recognition.
- **Hire differently**. My friend Bob hires for what he calls "the three A's": attitude, aptitude, and ability. Look for people who say "I can learn that" (attitude) instead of "That's not my job." Skills can be taught; humility and adaptability is what you're really hiring for.

These practices help build T-shaped team members who can handle multiple aspects of delivery. But the real power comes when you can systematically assess where your team needs these capabilities most.

From Where You Are to Where You're Going

Now that you understand the value of T-shaped team members, how do you identify which bottlenecks to tackle first? Start by mapping out what skills your team *needs* versus what they have. This reveals where people are overloaded (your bottlenecks) and where others are underutilized (your opportunities).

You don't require anything fancy—a simple "Skills and Strengths Assessment" shows you what experience is necessary (technical or otherwise) and where each team member stands. More importantly, this visual makes vulnerabilities obvious to leadership, helping you to confidently state the case for cross-training.

	Skills and Strengths Assessment							
	GitHub	**Jira**	**Postman**	**Docker**	**Slack**	**Jenkins**	**VS Code**	**Gaps to Address**
Dusty Back-End Dev	Green	Yellow	Green	Red	Yellow	Red	Yellow	Docker, Jenkins
Chase Front-End Dev	Yellow	Red	Yellow		Green		Green	Jira, Docker
Kyle Full Stack Dev	Green	Green	Green	Yellow	Green	Yellow	Green	Docker
Karissa Middle Layer Dev	Yellow	Yellow	Green	Yellow	Yellow	Red	Yellow	Jenkins
Casey Manual Tester	Red	Green	Yellow		Green		Red	VS Code, Docker
Laurel Automated Tester	Yellow	Green	Green	Red	Green	Yellow	Yellow	Docker, Jenkins

Skill Experience Key:

- Green: Proficient
- Yellow: Learning
- Red: Needs Training
- Blank: Beginner

This example shows each team member, their role, the tools needed to get work done, and where everyone lands:

- **Green = Proficient.** They know their stuff, work independently, and can help others or tackle complex problems.
- **Yellow = Learning.** They understand the basics and can do the work with some guidance and support.
- **Red = Needs Training.** They have minimal knowledge and can't work independently yet.
- **Blank = Beginner.** They may need to Google it first. (No shame in this, we've all been there!)

Why bother with this exercise? Well, because it reveals exactly where the project is vulnerable—like when only one person knows how to deploy code to production. It shows you where people can grow into more T-shaped contributors and which skills matter most for your team *right now*. Think of it as both a snapshot of where the team is today and a roadmap for getting stronger.

Critical side note—do not create this chart in isolation! I tried that once and presented my super awesome assessment to the team. Their expressions ranged from confused to "are you kidding me?" until I realized that I had accidentally shown the senior developer as "Red" in Java. The valuable lesson here: you need *your team's* honest input about *their own* skill level.

That's where the workshop comes in. It's a collaborative session where everyone helps build the map together, making the vulnerabilities impossible to ignore, and the solutions obvious to everyone involved.

Conduct this as a collective conversation where your PO provides the forecast of upcoming work. The development team identifies which tools they'll need and rates their own proficiency levels. When everyone builds this map together, gaps are immediately apparent. When guiding this workshop:

- **Be mindful of the team dynamics** and culture. This could be a sensitive subject, so a delicate approach may be necessary.

- **Frame the exercise positively**. This is a growth opportunity, not a performance review!
- **Use clear, objective skills levels** rather than subjective judgments. Rather than inferring that someone is "bad' at a particular skill, you can use phrases like "growth opportunity" or "skill development."
- **Look at this from a team perspective** by answering the question of: where would cross-training benefit *everyone*? This isn't about spotlighting the one person who's falling behind.
- **Prepare for pushback**. Some team members might resist this exercise if they've been burned by skill assessments before. Acknowledge this upfront and explain that this is not about judging expertise, it's about making sure that one person's vacation doesn't derail your entire sprint.

Helpful Tip: Start small. If the team seems hesitant, just focus on the most critical skills first. You don't have to map everything in one sitting. Repeat after me: Rome wasn't built in one day.

Once you've completed the assessment, use it to guide your T-shaped development efforts. Those yellow and red areas are *perfect* candidates for the lunch and learns, pair programming sessions, and learning days that we discussed in the table previously. The blank areas could be opportunities for someone to dive deep and teach others.

Remember, the goal is to build team effectiveness and identify learning opportunities. Done thoughtfully, this exercise brings the team together rather than creating division or discomfort. After all, we're simply mapping out where we are today so we can chart a course to where we need to be tomorrow. It's really that simple.

Your Teams Were Designed to Struggle

Thus far, I've been talking at length about building T-shaped teams and cross-functional collaboration, but as my friend Jim *looooooves* to inform me: *You know Kim, in reality, many organizations have purposely designed and implemented siloed teams* (specializing in front-end, or back-end, or data etc.) *and not cross-functional ones.*

This clearly conflicts with my dazzling (yet, dare I say, level headed) vision. And while I firmly believe that moving toward cross-functional teams capable of delivering complete vertical slices is **the** goal to strive for, I do recognize that we need to address this reality. So fine, let's discuss.

If you're working in an environment with specialized teams, here are a few approaches that can help them shift in the right direction:

- **Suggest combining team refinement sessions where the focus is on the epic, and not individual stories.** I'm imagining something like a user story map walkthrough, where the POs partner up to describe the epic (who's requesting it, why, and what outcomes they are looking for) and the definition of done.

  In this collaboration, team members from the various teams are discussing what needs to be done, in what order (sequential or parallel development), and what's needed for the work to start. These tasks are captured as the plan is taking shape. Ideally, although they may be separate teams, they are behaving as one with a common goal. This prevents misalignment and reduces the need for rework when all the components finally integrate.
- **Create a shared planning board.** (*Imagine old lady voice*) Back in "*my* day," when we all worked in the same building, we would write the tasks down on Post-it notes, arrange them on a huge wall, and draw lines between the stickies to denote dependencies. This provided the transparency into our strategy to anyone who may be interested. Plus, it gave us a solid anchor point for our daily discussions.

  Whether you use a physical surface, JIRA, or a whiteboarding tool like Miro, visualization of the work, ownership, due dates, and the dependencies between the work is crucial for shared understanding.
- **Establish cross-team communication channels.** Offer to coordinate and guide daily discussions, conduct joint team reviews, or implement regular sync-up meetings between

dependent teams. This tight alignment is critical when the organizational structure forces team dependencies.

⇧ *Now, Look Up!*

Why do organizations create these specialized silos in the first place? Usually it's not malicious—it's just misguided attempts to improve productivity. Here's what I've observed:

- **Perceived efficiency.** It's this mentality of "Why have every team learn database skills when we can have one database team serve everyone." (Spoiler alert, this creates massive bottlenecks.)
- **Scarcity mindset around specialized skills**. "We only have 3 database experts and 12 teams, so let's pool them together to keep them busy" rather than investing in growing broader capabilities across teams.
- **Expensive people should only do expensive work.** There's a common belief that high-paid specialists shouldn't "waste time" on anything outside their narrow expertise, so they get pooled together to focus on their unique specialist tasks.

So, what can you do, regardless of your authority? These are similar to the strategies we've been discussing throughout this book, applied specifically to specialized team challenges:

- **Document and present the bottleneck costs.** Track how long work sits waiting for the specialized team, how long the handoff and coordination takes, how long you wait to get it back, and then the inevitable bug fixes when things don't integrate smoothly. Put a shiny new price tag on that entire cycle and present it to leadership for review.
- **Challenge the "keep people busy" obsession.** *More tracking*? Yes, more data tracking! The key here is in explaining the negative impact of relying on external dependencies: "Yes, Katie, our database expert is 100 percent busy, but our last

five features took an extra two weeks each waiting for database work. That's 10 weeks of delayed customer value to keep one person fully busy." Follow this up with an experiment: "What if Katie was 100 percent dedicated to our team for one month, instead of spreading her out among 12 teams?"

- **Reframe specialist value.** Challenge the "expensive people should only do expensive work" mindset by helping leadership see the real return on investment (ROI): "When Katie only does database work, she's a bottleneck that delays five teams. When she can also help with testing and basic front-end work, she keeps two teams moving smoothly without any delays. Same salary, dramatically different business impact."

We all know that these approaches aren't replacements for truly cross-functional teams—they're just stepping stones on the path to better ways of working. But hey, it's better than nothing.

Why Your Tester Is Threatening to Quit

Many teams fall into what's commonly called the "waterfall sprint"—where development happens sequentially throughout the iteration, and testing gets compressed into the final day(s). If you've worked in agile for any length of time, you've likely experienced this antipattern and its consequences.

Consider the pattern of a typical 10-day waterfall iteration with 5 developers, 1 tester, and 10 stories:

- **Day one**: Each developer grabs two separate stories. The tester begins writing manual test cases.
- **Days two through nine**: The developers report: "I'm working on this story and that story, no blockers." The tester mentions that she "is available when something's ready for testing."
- **Day 10**: Suddenly, all developers announce: "Development complete; stories are ready for testing." The tester, now facing 10 stories to test in a single day, contemplates a career change to astronautics.

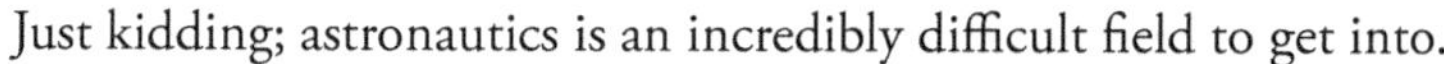

Just kidding; astronautics is an incredibly difficult field to get into.

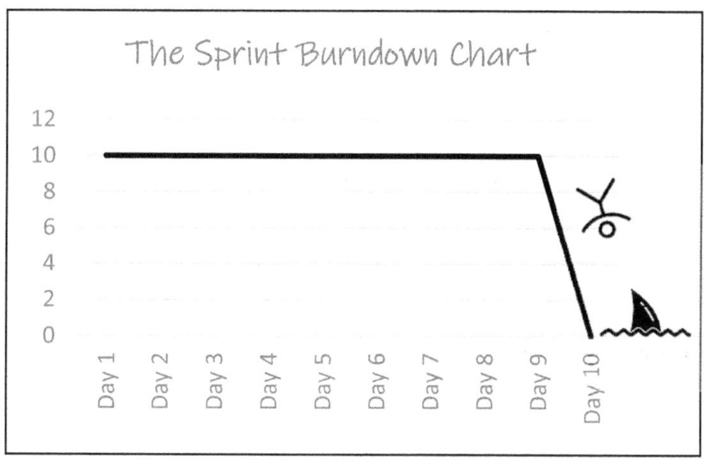

But the reality isn't much better—the tester works late into the night and through the weekend. Developers remain on call for inevitable bug fixes. The PO anxiously checks for show-stopping issues, while the delivery change agent watches the acceptance count, waiting to close the sprint. I believe this approach is straight up flawed because it:

- Leads to emotional and physical team burnout.
- Causes feedback loop delays.
- Compromises quality.
- Reduces opportunities for knowledge sharing and brainstorming.
- Hinders transparency about actual progress.
- Delays production as defects are found too late.

⇧ *Now, Look Up!*

From a systems perspective, what do you think is causing these waterfall sprints? Could it be:

- Cultures where individual busyness matters more than collective outcomes?
- Performance reviews that focus on individual accomplishments rather than team results?
- An entire organizational inability to limit WIP, across every level?

- External approval processes that prevent stories from reaching "Done" individually, forcing teams to batch their work?
- Or something else entirely?

A better approach?

Focus on completion, not individual productivity.

What if, instead of *each* developer focusing solely on only their assigned stories, **the *team* focused on getting the first couple of stories completely done before starting new work?** I can already hear the objections: *But, there's only one tester! What will developers do while waiting? This isn't efficient!* My answer is simple: *anyone* on the team can test, just not their *own* work.

Traffic Jam in the Test Lane

Suggesting that developers test is like asking your picky toddler to munch on an overcooked brussels sprout ("um, no thank you, but I *will* take that French fry"). Many developers have been taught that testing is "not their job," creating a mindset barrier that can be tougher to overcome than achieving world peace. The most common scenario plays out when development is complete and all the work falls to the overwhelmed tester (as we saw previously).

When I suggest that developers should test their colleagues' work, I often hear these counter points:

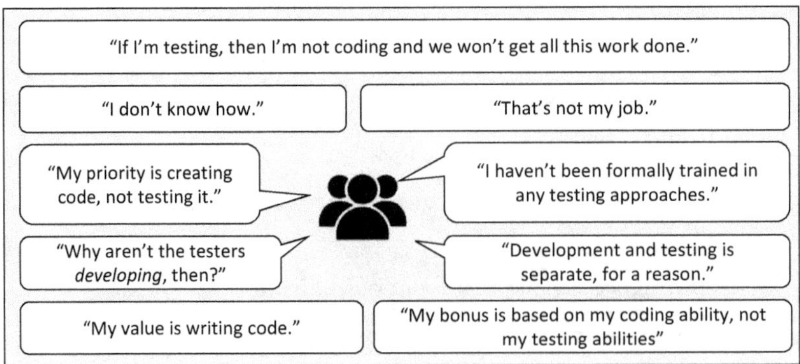

Before we jump into solutions, take a moment to look at these statements again. What organizational patterns do you think are creating these reactions?

- Which objections reveal misaligned incentives?
- What do these responses tell you about how roles are defined in your organization?
- Where do you see fears? What could be the root cause of these fears?
- Which objections suggest organizational silos rather than team collaboration?

Take a minute to think through these questions. I highly doubt these replies originate from individual stubbornness—they're usually symptoms of deeper organizational issues. Once you understand what's driving the potential resistance, you can address it more effectively.

- **Let the numbers do the talking.** Collect metrics that illustrate the testing bottleneck—stories waiting for QA, time spent in testing, defects found late, or weekend hours worked by testers.

  Present this information to the team without blame: "Here's what I'm seeing in our workflow. Your thoughts on this?" Let the data spark the conversation about how *the team* can support testing efforts.
- **Suggest that the team automate test scripts *together*.** Developers may resist manual testing but usually get excited about test automation. Pair developers with testers to build automated test suites—this tackles a key developer fear (that changes will break stuff) while spreading testing knowledge around the team.
- **Have honest conversations with managers about teamwork expectations.** Focus on business outcomes—faster delivery, better quality, and happier teams. Find out what *they* care about first. Are *they* measured on speed? Cost? Quality? Employee retention? Once you know their priorities, frame cross-functional collaboration as a way to achieve *their* goals.

This works when leadership is open-minded. But what about when they dig in their heels and insist that developers stay in their lane?

Help Others See What You See

Unfortunately, you may hit walls where leadership is hesitant about cross-functional collaboration. I've heard managers insist that "developers develop, testers test," and outright protest any blurring of these arbitrary boundaries. Welcome to organizational dysfunction 101.

First things first: recognize that these managers aren't being *intentionally* difficult. They often have legit reasons—maybe they've seen past cross-functional experiments crash and burn, or they're dealing with compliance requirements that demand clear role separation. But regardless of their rationale, you still need to work within this reality.

When faced with this kind of resistance, data becomes your most persuasive ally. Trust me, philosophical declarations around team dynamics and emotional dysfunction are perceived as hippy dippy nonsense. But real, tangible numbers showing business impact? Those get their attention fast.

Start by translating these invisible costs into language leadership fundamentally cares about—money, moola, and the green stuff—by documenting what's really happening with specific metrics.

Breaking Through Organizational Resistance: Your Three-Step Game Plan

Leadership doesn't care about your silly little processes or your theories—they care about results. Here's how to build a solid business case for cross-functional collaboration:

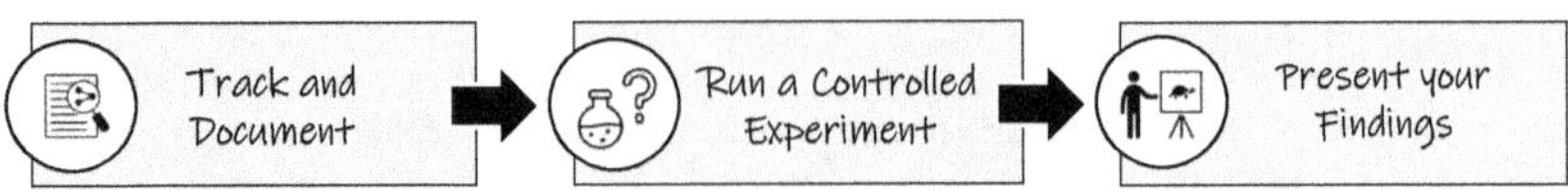

Step one: Track and document what's truly going on

- How long do stories sit around waiting for testing?
- How many overtime hours are testers putting in to finish everything?

- How many bugs are found in the final crunch? (To be more specific, "crunch" means the final 20 percent—so the last two days of a 10-day sprint.)
- What's the real cost difference? Bugs found early are much cheaper to fix than last-minute bugs, which require more time due to rushing, panic, and context switching.
- How long does it take for finished features to reach customers?

Seriously? Tracking this amount of data sounds tedious and time-consuming!

You're right, it absolutely is! And yeah, you'll need to be super consistent with this. But here's the unfortunate truth: as a change agent, you *need* compelling evidence in order to shift outdated perspectives.

Data isn't a "nice to have"—it's your most influential tool for creating meaningful change.

I promise, the short-term pain pays off tremendously when you can present your case with confidence rather than intuition or ideology.

Step two: Run a controlled experiment

For just one iteration, try a more collaborative approach where developers test throughout the sprint. Measure the same stuff and compare the results. Usually, you'll see dramatic improvements in cycle time, quality, and predictability.

Step three: Present your findings in terms that resonate with leadership

Talk about business value—faster delivery, better quality, and lower costs. For example:

- "Our testers are working nights and weekends every sprint just to keep up. We're burning them out, which means more mistakes and higher turnover risk. Meanwhile, developers have moved on to next iteration's work, so when bugs inevitably come back, it's disruptive and expensive to fix."

- "Features sit finished but untested for over a week. That means customers are waiting for stuff we've already built. We're delaying feedback and slowing down our ability to improve."
- "In the sprint where developers pitched in with testing, we caught most bugs immediately and didn't have a single tester working overtime. The entire team could have dinner with their families on release day."

Remember, focus on shared goals, not process theory. Talk about cross-functional collaboration in terms of *real* business benefits, not some fluffy team-building concept. Show them the money they're wasting, not your precious methodology.

Helpful Tip: If they're still not convinced, try small changes that don't require formal approval. Maybe developers and testers pair on a complex feature. Or you can introduce "bug bash" sessions where the whole team tests for an hour. These micro steps often prove value without setting off organizational alarms.

If frustration overwhelms you ("Argh! Why does it always feel like I'm pushing a boulder uphill?"), take a deep breath and assume positive intent. Their resistance usually comes from valid concerns—productivity worries, belief in specialization benefits, or career development fears. They're not being "antiagile" or personally attacking you (although it may feel like that). You just have different ideas about what success looks like.

If they're *still* not budging after seeing all your evidence, here's what might be going on:

- There are legitimate reasons specialized roles work better in your environment (like heavy regulatory compliance).
- The timing might suck for this kind of change.
- The culture might not be ready yet (or … ever).
- They might have bigger fish to fry.

When that happens, focus your energy where you can make a difference. Keep tracking what this dysfunction is costing them, and be ready to make your case when the right moment arrives.

Finally, pick your battles. Even bite-sized improvements can create real value for the team and build your credibility for bigger changes later.

And you know what? Let's be perfectly real here—you may *never* convince some people that testing is a team sport. Know when to cut your losses and call it a day.

From Uncomfortable Threat to Acceptable Experiment

Humans hate being forced to change. We're hardwired to find it uncomfortable, scary, and downright unnerving. Expect to be met with resistance, awkward silence, or occasionally, red-faced fury when you suggest trying something new.

Stop "implementing changes" and start "running experiments" instead.

When you frame a new idea as an experiment, you instantly lower the stakes. People who would normally dig their heels in against permanent change will often shrug and say, "Sure, we can try that for a week" *because* its only temporary.

The beauty of experiments is that they're impermanent by definition. They have a clear start, clear end, and an evaluation period. They give the team a safe space to test drive new ways of working without committing to them *forever*. Knowing that makes people feel more in control—they know there's an exit strategy if things go sideways.

I've witnessed teams' revolt at the suggestion of a new process, then participate when framed as an experiment: "Let's experiment with this for one iteration and then decide together if it's worth continuing." **The "E" word transforms change from a threat into an opportunity for discovery.**

Six Questions That Save You From Bad Ideas

Another common obstacle I see is that teams and individuals *jump straight to solutions* without clearly defining the problem. This is like requesting medication without first diagnosing the illness.

Can you imagine walking into your physician's office and saying "Hey doc, write me a prescription for antibiotics" without explaining your symptoms? Your doctor would have *no* idea if antibiotics are even appropriate for what's ailing you.

Yet this is exactly what happens in our teams. "We need to automate our testing!" sounds lovely, but if your real issue is poorly defined requirements, automation will just help you build the wrong thing faster.

Why do you think teams jump straight to solutions? I find it's often because organizations reward action (doing) over analysis (thinking). When leaders ask "What's the plan?" instead of "What problem are we solving?" teams learn to propose quick fixes rather than dig deep into the root causes.

To avoid this trap, take the time to nail down the real issue before communicating your idea. The "Problem Identification Worksheet" includes six simple questions that help you figure out what's *truly* wrong before you start proposing fixes. Work through these questions, and you'll bring a solid, well-thought-out idea to your team instead of just another random solution looking for a problem (there's enough of those already).

The Problem Identification Worksheet

Question	Example
What do you want to fix?	Customer requirements are unclear and everyone understands them differently.
What's going wrong right now?	Team members build different things because we're all guessing what the customer actually wants. This leads to rework, missed deadlines, and frustrated people.
What's your guess about how to fix it?	If we sketch out what we're building together before anyone starts coding, we'll stop building the wrong stuff —at least half the time.
How will you test your guess?	For the next sprint, we'll spend an hour sketching out each big story before anyone starts working on it. The product owner draws what they're thinking, and we all ask questions about any weird edge cases.
How will you know if it worked?	• Count how many bugs come from building the wrong thing • Ask the team: "Are requirements clearer now?" (1-5 scale) • Track how long stories take from start to finish
What might get in the way?	• Finding time when everyone can actually meet • Product owner might hate drawing/sketching • Might feel slower at first even if it saves time later

- **What do you want to fix?** This is your problem statement—so get specific about what's happening. Instead of *There is confusion as to what the customer needs* (vague) try *Customer requirements are unclear and inconsistently understood across the team* (explicit!).
- **What's going on right now?** Jumping back to the medical analogy mentioned previously, what symptoms are you feeling? What is the impact of this situation—to the team, an individual, the organization?
- **What's your guess about how to fix it?** Form a clear if/then statement by stating your tests, assumptions, and the why: ***If*** *we create and review visual mockups together before development begins,* ***then*** *we'll reduce requirement misunderstandings by at least 50 percent.*
- **How will you test your guess?** When designing your experiment, keep it simple and focused on testing just one change at a time—this clarity helps you know exactly what worked or didn't. Also, the goal isn't to prove your hypothesis right *(although omg, that's* ***so*** *very satisfying when it happens)*; it's to learn something useful regardless of the outcome.
- **How will you know if it worked?** Choose measurements that will **clearly** indicate success or failure. Make sure you capture the current state of these metrics before starting the experiment—you can't prove that something improved if you can't prove where you started.
- **What might get in the way?** This is where brainstorming comes in handy. What could essentially cause your experiment to go awry? By calling out these risks, you can proactively discuss mitigation strategies.

One final thought—don't fill this out in isolation at your desk. Use it as a conversation starter with your team (or manager, colleague, and business partners). You might be surprised by what problems *they* want to solve.

Swarming Isn't Just for Bees

Have you ever watched a nature documentary showing honeybees clustering together in a humming mass of synchronized purpose? That's swarming—nature's way of saying "we're better together than apart." While bees swarm to establish new colonies, teams swarm to crush impediments and get stuff done.

If your team hasn't tried swarming yet, they're missing out on one of the most powerful techniques for attacking bottlenecks and finishing what they started. (Remember our mantra from earlier: "Stop starting, start finishing," that's the goal.)

When I talk about "swarming," I'm not suggesting that the team buzzes around aimlessly. I mean multiple team members are laser focused on completing a single story as quickly as possible. It's the antidote to the "waterfall" disaster we discussed earlier. Instead of everybody working on their own separate stories (creating that testing tsunami at sprint end), the team collaborates to drive one high priority item across the finish line before tackling the next.

This works beautifully when you've got those vertically sliced stories that deliver business value and can generate real feedback from users.

Swarming transforms your daily meetings from mind-numbing status updates ("I worked on X yesterday, I'll work on Y today, no blockers") into dynamic dialog: "We're making great progress on the payment feature, but we've hit a snag with the API integration. Laurel, can you help Casey troubleshoot this while Dusty and I finalize the UI?"

So, what does swarming look like when you strip away the buzzwords and get down to the nitty-gritty?

How to Team Up Without Chaos

During iteration planning, after the team commits to their stories and discusses the "how," they create tasks that represent distinct chunks of work needed to complete each story.

Small Tasks = Big Momentum

Here's where many teams stumble—they create massive tasks like "Development" that drag on for days with no visible progress. Nope! Keep those tasks small enough to complete in one business day or less.

Why would I say this? Because there's nothing *more* motivating than moving something from "Doing" to "Done," and nothing more *demoralizing* than seeing the same task stuck in progress for days on end.

Plus, it creates transparency—if something's taking longer than expected, you'll know right away rather than discovering it three days later.

Then when the iteration kicks off, pay close attention to the first daily meeting. Instead of everyone grabbing their own stories, several team members volunteer to tackle that top priority item together. Maybe two developers pair on the back-end while another tackles the UI, with a tester creating automation scripts in parallel. They self-select the tasks, forming a collaborative group that's laser focused on getting that story done.

Once that first story has enough people working on it, the remaining team members review the next highest priority item and repeat the process. This continues until everyone has meaningful work **for the day**—not the entire sprint.

Now, don't over plan! Focus on getting those top one to three stories moving, not on assigning every task (or story) for the entire iteration. Embrace your lean thinking mindset and recognize that detailed planning of day eight's work on day one is just *wasteful.* The iteration will unfold in ways you can't predict, so stay flexible and focused on what's immediately ahead.

The transformation I've seen when teams adopt swarming is remarkable. That subtle but profound shift from "my work" to "our work" changes literally *everything*:

- Suddenly, shared accountability replaces blame.
- Isolation surrenders to collaboration.
- Knowledge flows freely rather than being buried in silos.
- And perhaps most importantly, stuff gets DONE instead of lingering at 80 percent complete.

Swarming fundamentally changes how teams approach their work, shifting from "my task" (me) to "our goal" (we). When combined with the other practices we've discussed—eliminating SPOFs, developing T-shaped team members, breaking the waterfall pattern, and embracing experimentation—it creates a powerful formula for product acceleration. This, my friends, is pure gold.

⇧ *Now, Look Up!*

OK, so you've tried to encourage swarming and are met with resistance. Team members *insist* on working individually, managers want to track who did what. What organizational patterns might be creating this?

- The system rewards individual heroics over team success.
- Performance reviews that ask "What did *you* accomplish?" instead of "How did you help *the team* succeed?" train people to hoard work and take individual credit.
- Managers who assign stories to specific people before the iteration even starts are signaling that individual ownership matters more than collective outcomes.

These are the same organizational dysfunctions we've been tackling throughout this book—and the same strategies (visibility, celebration of team wins, cost documentation, and team-focused metrics) apply here. Swarming, T-shaped team members, experimentation, and all the other practices in this chapter work best when the organizational system **supports** them rather than fights them.

These aren't just nice to have practices; they're essential tools for removing the waste that's keeping your product from reaching enthusiastic customers. By identifying and addressing these inefficiencies, you transform your team from a robotic assembly line to a collaborative force that consistently delivers value.

Connect the Dots and Take Action

Throughout this chapter, we've tackled the big things that slow teams down:

- **When one person knows everything** and becomes a critical bottleneck (*like Susie who couldn't take vacation*).
- **The "that's not my job" mentality** that creates handoffs and delays (*solved by building T-shaped teams that can swarm on problems*).
- **Waterfall sprints** where testing becomes a last-day nightmare (*fixed by focusing on Stop Starting! Start Finishing!*).
- **People who resist trying anything new,** keeping those bad habits in place (*overcome by framing changes as experiments*).
- **Waste hiding everywhere** in your organization (*spotted using the DOWNTIME framework*).

And you've also been given the tools (like the DOWNTIME model) to spot and eliminate these problems systematically.

- Defects that require rework and damage your company's reputation.
- Overproduction that creates features nobody asked for.
- Waiting for approvals and decisions that crush productivity.
- Non-utilized talent that wastes people's knowledge and skills.
- Transportation that shuffles information unnecessarily between systems.
- Inventory of work that piles up without delivering value.
- Motion from repetitive manual tasks that could be automated.
- Excess processing that gold-plates simple problems with overly complex solutions.

Keep in mind—waste isn't always obvious. It often hides in plain sight, disguised as "the way we've always done it" or "best practices" that aren't ... best (*or even good*). You're perfectly positioned to make these invisible inefficiencies visible and to help the team eliminate them.

One final thought: this isn't a one-and-done effort—the work of removing waste is *never* complete. But with each waste you eliminate, you'll see delivery speed increase, team morale improve, and the ability to meet your customer needs strengthen.

Here's my challenge for you

Cool, so what now? Well, you've got two places to focus your efforts:

- On your team.
- On your organization.

On Your Team:

Your Team Influence Plan			
1 **START WITH AWARENESS** Share the DOWNTIME waste categories with your team and lead the conversation about which ones are sabotaging their daily work. Run a "waste safari" where everyone hunts for examples of each type of waste.	2 **PICK ONE WASTE TO ADDRESS FIRST** Don't try to boil the ocean. Pick the waste that's both driving everyone crazy and it's something you can actually do something about.	3 **DESIGN A SMALL EXPERIMENT** Use the Problem Identification Worksheet to figure out how to attack that waste. Keep it small, give it a deadline, and make sure you can actually measure if it worked.	3 **COLLECT DATA (BEFORE, DURING, AFTER)** Numbers speak louder than opinions, especially when you're trying to convince skeptical stakeholders.
4 **FOCUS RETROSPECTIVES ON WASTE REDUCTION** Ask directed questions: What waste did we actually eliminate this iteration? What waste is still driving us nuts? What should we try next?	5 **CELEBRATE AND SHARE SUCCESSES** When an experiment works, make some noise about it! Tell other teams who might be dealing with the same frustrations.	6 **GRADUALLY EXPAND YOUR FOCUS** Once you've conquered one type of waste, go after the next biggest pain point.	7 **PREVENT WASTE FROM RETURNING** Lock in those awesome wins by updating your Definition of Done, working agreements, or whatever team practices need tweaking so the waste doesn't sneak back in.

On Your Organization:

Your Organizational Influence Plan			
1 **MAP THE SYSTEM** Figure out what's *really* going on. Who actually makes the decisions that block the flow? What encourages individual heroics over team collaboration? Where do all these competing priorities come from anyway?	2 **QUANTIFY THE IMPACT** Put a price tag on the dysfunction. Track how long stuff sits waiting for approvals, calculate what context switching actually costs, and document what happens when *everything* is "high priority."	3 **FIND YOUR ALLIES** Look for leaders who are already frustrated with the same crap you're seeing. Partner with managers who get it. Build relationships with people who can actually change things.	4 **MAKE THE PROBLEMS VISIBLE** Show them the data in language they care about—lost money, missed deadlines, good people quitting. Focus on patterns, not just individual "oops" moments.
5 **PROPOSE SMALL EXPERIMENTS** Suggest lightweight changes that don't threaten existing power structures (or fragile egos). Test your ideas: "What could happen if we picked our top 3 priorities and stuck with them for a month?"	6 **CELEBRATE SYSTEM WINS** When organizational changes work (and they absolutely will!), shout it from the rooftops! Show leadership how fixing *the system* led to better results.	7 **SCALE WHAT WORKS** Take the good stuff and spread it around to other teams or departments. Use your success stories to build momentum for bigger changes.	8 **STAY PATIENT STAY PERSISTENT** Changing an organization is like turning the Titanic—slow and cumbersome. Keep documenting the problems and pushing for solutions, even when it feels like you're talking to a brick wall.

Remember, reducing waste *isn't* about working harder—it's about removing the obstacles that prevent people from doing their best work. Some of those obstacles live at the team level, others are baked into how your organization operates. When you eliminate the drag of inefficiency (*remember those barnacles!*) at both levels, you'll be amazed at how quickly things can move.

Looking Ahead

We've covered a lot of ground on fixing team and organizational problems. But here's something else that I've learned the hard way—sometimes the biggest obstacle to getting things done isn't a broken process or stubborn leadership.

Sometimes it's you. (*Or rather, it was me.*)

You *can't* control whether your organization will embrace T-shaped teams, address the DOWNTIME waste, or stop rewarding individual heroes. But you absolutely *can* control how *you* show up, how you react when things go sideways, and whether *you* make a situation better or worse.

The next chapter is completely different from everything we've talked about so far. We're going inward with the focus on how to manage yourself—so you can be more effective at managing everything else. We'll cover:

- How to receive feedback without falling apart.
- What *really* drives you.
- Staying curious instead of getting judgmental.
- Keeping your cool during conflict.
- Knowing when to pick your battles.

Because here's the thing: all those techniques for eliminating waste and building better teams *only* work if you can implement them *without creating more chaos.*

CHAPTER 7

The Reawakening—Building Your Foundation for Success

Congrats, you've made it this far! You've learned how to improve customer satisfaction, make work visible, eliminate waste, and accelerate delivery. You've got what it takes—the skills, the frameworks, and the tools—to be an exceptional delivery change agent. But none of that matters if you can't get out of your *own* way first.

In my years of coaching and mentoring, I've watched brilliant professionals flounder—not because they lacked knowledge, but because they couldn't control their own emotions, maintain presence in arduous conversations, or recognize when their ego consumed them.

Introspection isn't only reserved for creek side meditation retreats. It's the foundation that makes *everything else* in this book possible. You can learn every process, tool, or technique by heart, but if you can't manage your triggers, maintain your cool, or understand what's truly going on within yourself, you'll never reach your full potential.

When looking inside, we must look deep within. We need awareness of our patterns, the ability to regulate our responses, and the discipline to change what isn't working. It means asking ourselves hard questions: Am I truly walking my talk, or just ... talking to talk? Do I champion curiosity but rarely ask inquisitive questions myself? Do I feel unheard but fail to listen intently to others? Do I expect behaviors from others that I haven't modeled myself?

This chapter gets personal (and I get vulnerable). It asks you to gaze inward with the same analytical mind you bring to organizational improvements. It challenges you to apply this continuous improvement mindset to yourself. And yes, it might make you uncomfortable—but keep in mind, growth is born from discomfort.

This is the type of work that will transform you from good to exceptional. This is what will sustain you when the job gets tough. This is what will enable you to create the impact you're capable of making.

When Feedback Feels Like an Attack

I've worked with some incredible coaches over the years—people I deeply respect who've become mentors, allies, and friends. Much of my success comes from their influence and support. So, why is it that I stiffen when one of them innocently asks "Hey, can I give you feedback?"

That one harmless question violently wakes up this insecure, timid child buried deep into my psyche. Upon hearing this innocent offer, she immediately squeezes her eyes shut, covers her ears, and shouts "NOOO! NO! NO! I DON'T WANT TO HEAR YOUR FEEDBACK!"

So, look, here's the thing. I don't want to hear their observations because I automatically assume that it will be a negative attack on my character. Regardless of how pleasantly the commentary is given, the underlying message will always translate in my mind to "you're not good enough."

But okay, let's be real. ***How can I provide observations and guidance to others if I cannot welcome (much less accept) input myself?*** (And also, like, what's my deal?)

The disconnect between what I preach and what I practice isn't just hypocritical—it's a fundamental barrier to my effectiveness as a coach and leader. After all, if I can't model the behaviors I'm advocating, why would anyone follow my guidance? These perspectives are the mirror that shows us not just *what* we're doing, but how we're being perceived. And like actual mirrors on hot humid days, sometimes we'd rather just not look.

Through my work with the Shirzad Chamine's Positive Intelligence Program (really cool course, I highly recommend), I discovered that one of my primary saboteurs—the devious internal voice that sabotages our best intentions—is the "Hyper-Achiever." This means I'm naturally competitive and image/status conscious. I strive to maintain a tight lid on my insecurities, terrified that others will see through the "picture perfect" image I work so hard to project. By opening myself to others' perspectives, I'm forced to confront the reality I've been avoiding: that I am a messy, anxious, flawed human.

Just like everyone else.

And it was this revelation, this unveiling of my "Hyper-Achiever" saboteur, that allowed me to confront this part of myself. Has this shiny new internal knowledge fixed everything? Nope, absolutely not. Embracing my imperfections is literally, a lifelong battle. But now, I can at least see feedback through the lens of my saboteur, and not undeniable fact.

As delivery change agents, we often struggle to receive the very input we encourage others to embrace. This creates a conundrum where our fear blocks our growth. Here are a few ideas to transform your relationship with critique from fear to receptivity:

- **Go deep.** If your mentor, role model, or teacher walks up to you and says "Hey, can I give you feedback?," what will be your *initial* reaction? If it's anything other than "Oh, for sure!," ask yourself the following two questions: "What's stopping me from openly receiving this feedback?" and … "What am I afraid of?" Then follow those answers up with a few whys, to get to the heart of the matter. Knowledge is power, and knowing yourself is the first step toward reclaiming your courage.
- **Invest in yourself.** Consider working with a coach, taking a self-awareness assessment, or exploring programs that help you understand your internal patterns and what triggers your defensiveness. Understanding your specific triggers—whether it's perfectionism, people-pleasing, or something else—gives you the power to recognize and manage them.
- **Reframe it.** If someone has:
  a) taken an interest in your success,
  b) been truly present with you (not just offering cheap drive-by critiques),
  c) noted any possible blind spots or areas of opportunities,
  d) courageously offered their recommendations to you, or
  e) provided their feedback in a nonjudgmental, loving manner, then it stands to reason that they are looking out for your best interests; they are attempting to lift you higher. Shifting your perspective from "I'm being attacked" to "I'm being seen as worthy of growth" can transform how you receive feedback.

- **Develop a powerful mantra.** This could be a simple phrase you can use to counterattack those overwhelming, deceitful, nasty insecurities. Something like: "This feedback is about my work, not my worth" or "This person cares about my growth and wants me to succeed."
- **Communicate how you like feedback to be given to you.** I prefer the poop sandwich: tell me something positive (delicious crispy bread) + then tell me what you've observed (maple honey ham and baby Swiss cheese) + another positive comment (more delicious crispy bread). I also require tangible examples that help me sort through what realistically occurred, versus what could have taken place (if I had done or said something differently). How would you like *your* feedback communicated?

What about when *you're* the one giving feedback? Turns out your motives matter just as much as your words.

Your Ego Is Lying to You

The most dangerous lies are the ones we tell ourselves about why we're doing what we're doing. Our motives shape *everything*—how we speak, how we act, how others receive our messages—yet they often remain deeply hidden, even from ourselves. I discovered this truth the hard way, when what I thought was helpful feedback was my wounded ego in disguise.

I was the scrum master for a team who considered themselves rock stars. Every retrospective: "There's nothing we need to improve. We kick ass!" My product owner didn't believe that the team needed a scrum master and rejected most of my suggestions.

This was something I took extremely personally and my frAgile ego was bent, gnarled, in ruins. I had something to prove—I was going to find just *one* thing I could remedy to justify my existence and demonstrate my value.

And I found it: no test automation. Perfect! I could fix this, save the team significant time, and finally validate my worth. But instead of approaching it with curiosity—asking "why is test automation missing?"—I made assumptions: "the developers were lazy, they didn't care about testing, they thought it was beneath them." Armed with this superior narrative and my wounded pride, I confronted the team on our next call, raising my concern about their lack of test automation with accusatory, irritated energy.

My behavior was so disrespectful that I brought the normally calm lead developer to fury. He shouted, I retaliated, he disconnected from the call. Then came my complete unraveling—fat, embarrassed tears as I realized the ugly truth: my comments hadn't been about helping the team at all. This was only about validating my own worth.

I eventually learned something humbling: they wanted test automation but were technically unable to implement it due to hardware constraints. This wasn't a people problem—it was a system problem. I felt smaller than ever.

Later, my manager Nelda asked a question that changed everything: "How could this have been different if you had assumed positive intent?" In that moment, I realized I was pushing an agenda that was rooted in fear, and insecurity, not love. **My motive wasn't to serve the team—it was to serve myself.**

This cycle is predictable and destructive: when our value feels threatened, we shift into self-protection mode, devise stories about others' intentions, and offer "help" with strings attached, damaging the very relationships we need most.

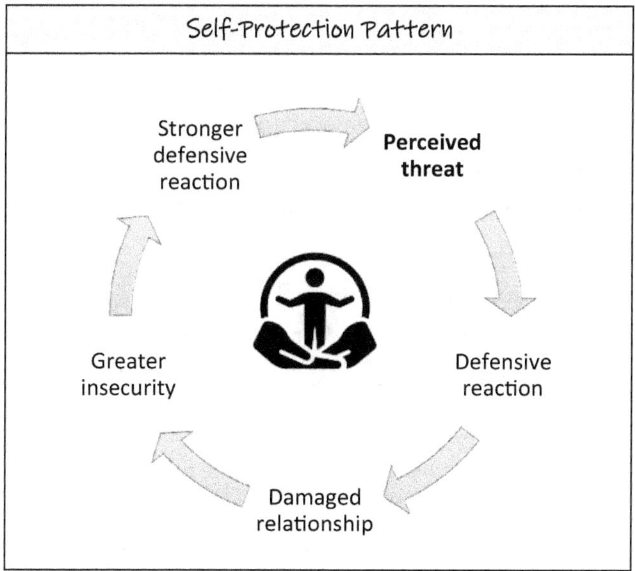

Breaking this cycle begins with one critical skill: the ability to recognize and honestly name those indisputable motivations. When facing internal conflict, take a breath, look deep within, and understand your core incentives. If it's anything but love, step back, and reevaluate.

Motive Check—Questions to Ask Yourself Before Giving Feedback

- **Check your intentions.** Before offering feedback or pushing an agenda, ask yourself: "Who am I really serving with this action—the person, the team, the project, or my own ego?" If it's the latter, put the feedback on pause, and turn your reflections inward.
- **Run the "love or fear" test.** Ask yourself: Do my actions, thoughts, words, or intent come from a place of love, or a place of fear? If it's anything but love, consider choosing contemplative silence over ego-driven reactions.
- **Put yourself in their shoes.** Ask "How would I feel receiving this feedback in the way I'm planning to deliver it?" If you'd feel defensive, your approach probably needs to be tweaked.
- **Seek out validation.** Ask a trusted colleague or mentor to help you examine your true motives. Sometimes we need an external mirror in order to see our blind spots more clearly.

When we honestly examine our deeply held motives, we often discover that beneath our defensiveness and need to prove ourselves lies something far more powerful: our innate curiosity. That same curiosity that once had us asking "why?" to everything as children—before we learned to protect our egos and assert our expertise.

In my test automation story, what if I had approached the situation not from a place of wounded pride, but genuine wonder? What if, instead of making assumptions about the team's motivations, I had simply been curious?

The Curious Person's Advantage

In the abovementioned story, I made way too many hostile assumptions. Never once did I ask the team why test automation was missing. It didn't dawn on me to maybe … I don't know, *take a stance of curiosity*? Nope, as mentioned previously, I was there to prove my worth and that was my only target.

Taking a step back, how could the situation have played out, if I had approached the team from an inquisitive mindset instead? Starting with my observations and then using open ended questions (questions that do not allow for a simple yes or no answer) would have been a better start. For example:

State my observation using nonjudgmental, unemotional language*: I notice this team spends roughly 27 percent of the sprint executing manual test cases.*

Followed up with open-ended, supportive questions:

- *What are your thoughts on that?*
- *What ideas do you have to make this process more efficient?*
- *How might we decrease this time?*

Some people get hung up on these types of questions: *What if my question isn't the most impactful, perfect, or powerful question there is?*

Don't stress over finding the perfect powerful question to ask, that's not the point. The point is to remain intentionally curious, asking questions from an honest space of wonder and fascination. Any question that originates from this space *is* the ideal question.

How Curious Are You?

Here's an experiment to gauge your base curiosity level: grab two pieces of paper. At the top of one, title it "Statements Made" on the other, title it "Questions Asked." For one full day, keep track of the number of statements you make versus the questions you ask.

Afterward, reflect on your numbers. What did you learn? Look at your "statements made" to "questions asked" ratio—was it 10:1? 20:1? How frequently did you make assumptions, and how many of those turned out to be false? (Be honest!) How often did you inform or tell rather than inquire or challenge? Consider how the communication might have improved if you'd switched even *half* of those statements to questions.

When I first performed this exercise, I was astounded by my general lack of inquiry. Upon further reflection, I noticed that I relied on my various beliefs, generalized presumptions, and internal biases to either move the conversation forward, or kill it altogether. My focus was on meeting efficiency, rather than human to human communication.

If there's one thing I've learned, it's that curiosity isn't a "nice-to-have" quality—it's the backbone of innovation, connection, and growth.

When we approach situations with genuine wonder rather than predetermined judgments, we open doorways to possibilities we might otherwise miss. Here is where I challenge you to reclaim your childlike curiosity:

- **Create a "Curiosity Journal."** At the end of each day, write down three things you're genuinely curious about—from your work, your relationships, or the world around you. Then pick one to explore more deeply tomorrow.
- **Practice saying "Help me understand."** I learned this from Chris, a fantastic coach and friend. When someone shares an idea or perspective different from his, rather than immediately responding with his own thoughts, he would simply say, "Help me understand more about that." It's amazing how this small phrase opens conversations, and strengthens relationships, in remarkable ways.
- **Direct the "Five Whys" on yourself.** When you feel strongly about something (*especially* when you're about to dig in your heels) ask yourself why you believe it, then why that's true, and keep going with the "why's" until you find the root. Often our strongest opinions have the weakest foundations.

What would have been possible if I had led from curiosity rather than assumption? Almost anything! But curiosity alone isn't enough. Even the most inquisitive mind can be derailed when emotions take over. This is where the next challenge emerges: learning to manage our emotional responses so they enhance, rather than hijack our effectiveness.

From Emotional Meltdown to Emotional Control

At this point, most of us have heard about "Emotional Intelligence (EQ)," which is defined as the "ability to understand, use, and manage your own emotions in positive ways to relieve stress, communicate effectively, empathize with others, overcome challenges, and defuse conflict."

Managing your inner responses is crucial, in both a professional and personal context. This is the fluffy stuff that gets brushed aside in most workplaces, but is totally necessary. This kind of self-awareness will get you far in life. It will enable you to build and foster strong relationships, inspire confidence in others, bounce back from life's curve balls, and navigate conflicts with grace. I believe that EQ is what separates people who *just survive* from people who *truly thrive.*

Picture someone you admire—not just professionally, but as a complete human being. When you think of this person, what do you notice? How do they hold themselves? Consider their mannerisms, the expression on their face, and the tone of their voice. What words do they choose? What assumptions are you making about them, and how do you feel in their presence?

During this activity, my mind turns to David, my mentor, coach, and friend, who is the most emotionally intelligent person I know. He speaks cautiously, thoughtfully, and powerfully. His words are precise, his tone soft, his essence open. He draws you in with carefully crafted questions and when you answer, he leans forward, listening intently, and making you feel like *what you just said matters.* He's never raised his voice or brought anyone to tears.

I wish I could say the same about myself. While David represents this composure at its finest, my own journey has been far messier and is far from over. I've been an absolute jerk at times, leaving emotional wreckage that still makes me cringe when I recall it. Even now, I catch myself slipping into old patterns. The difference is that I recognize them faster, recover more quickly, and repair any damage more sincerely. Those painful wake-up calls were necessary medicine, and I'm still taking regular doses.

Here are a few examples. I once angrily informed a colleague that no one on the team liked him. On a separate occasion, a product owner ran out of the meeting room in tears, due to the harshness of my message, of my tone. Conversations switched to epic battles when I felt the need to win. I would proudly argue with anyone on any topic that I was convinced I was right about. I spoke over people, shut down others, or ignored them altogether.

Clearly, I had work to do. Through painful trial and error (major emphasis on painful), I've learned some practices that helped transform my knee-jerk reactions. If you're ready to move from explosive to serene, here are the techniques that saved me from myself:

- **Create your emotional dashboard.** Just as cars have gauges to monitor speed and fuel, develop awareness of what's happening inside you. Several times daily, ask: "What am I feeling right now? Where do I feel it in my body? What triggered it?" The simple act of *noticing* these reactions gives you power over them.
- **Name it.** When feelings flood your system, simply labeling them ("I'm feeling resentful") helps to reduce the intensity. Use a variation of the "feelings wheel" to expand your emotional vocabulary beyond the basics—are you irritated, exasperated, or indignant? Each has different nuances worth exploring.
- **Develop a personal pause button.** Create a trigger phrase that reminds you to breathe before responding. Mine is "that's interesting, can you provide additional context?"—it buys me precious seconds to check myself before replying. Your phrase might be "let me consider that" or "I appreciate you sharing that."

- **Seek feedback from your truth-tellers.** Identify people who will lovingly call you on your ~~bullshit~~ emotional blind spots. My mentor Cory and I agreed on a subtle signal system—he would simply touch a finger to his nose whenever I started micromanaging the team. That silent, prearranged feedback was more powerful than *any* lecture.

The journey toward self-mastery isn't about never feeling intensely—it's about ensuring that your reactions *enhance* rather than *hijack* your effectiveness. In a profession where relationships are everything, this might be the most valuable skill you'll ever develop.

But even with all these tools and awareness, I still found myself getting triggered and jumping into unnecessary battles. That's when I learned the most important lesson of all—not every fight is worth fighting.

Some Oranges Aren't Worth Squeezing

- *The stories are split horizontally because that's how the team likes to work.*
- *We don't need a sprint goal.*
- *The back-end developers work on a separate team.*

Feel that knot in your stomach? That rush of heat to your face? These statements used to trigger my inner scrum snob faster than free pizza disappears from a break room. With my well-worn scrum guide practically fused to my palm, I'd launch into battle mode.

When they'd say "Developers don't test. We have testers for that," I'd fire back with "Team members should be T-shaped and cross-functional! You're all responsible for testing!" If someone dared mention "This is how we've always done it," I'd deliver an audible sigh followed by "That doesn't mean you should."

Every conversation became a correctional lecture. Every deviation from the scrum guide became a hill to die on. And, God, it was so exhausting. I had turned every inadequacy into a hill to die on.

If everything's a fight, then nothing is.

I remember venting to my colleague Rosemary, "They don't do ANYTHING by the book! This team is a disaster. Just imagine the value they could deliver if they'd follow proper scrum!"

She listened patiently, nodding with empathy, until I finally paused for a breath. Then she simply asked: "Is the juice worth the squeeze?"

Six words that stopped me in my tracks.

Is
the
juice
worth
the
squeeze?

Or said more plainly: **Is the outcome worth the effort?** Does the potential reward justify the energy, time, and relationship capital I was burning through?

Think about it: We juice oranges because they're literally bursting with liquid gold. But a banana? Have you ever had banana juice? No, because you'd get nothing but chunky mush. All that squeezing—wasted effort. Before launching into battle mode, I ask myself: Am I squeezing...

- ... A juicy orange that will yield something refreshing and nourishing? Or
- ... A banana that will leave me with nothing but sticky fingers and frustration?

This mental pause gives me space to decide if the fight is worth fighting. Because sometimes it's best if the banana just ... stays a banana.

If you're ready to stop exhausting yourself by squeezing every conceptual banana that crosses your path, here are some practices that have saved me countless hours of annoyance:

- **Apply the TMMY rule.** Before rushing into battle, ask yourself: Will this matter in 10 minutes? 10 months? 10 years? Most issues that seem critical in the moment shrink dramatically with this perspective check.

- **Create a "worth fighting for" checklist.** Identify your non-negotiables—the core principles that matter to you. For example, when I consider delivery, what matters is psychological safety, clear outcomes, and sustainable pace. Everything else? Negotiable. This gives you a quick filter for potential battles.
- **Track your wins-to-effort ratio.** After each "fight" (or "round"), note what you invested (time, political capital, emotional energy, reputational risk) and what changed as a result. Patterns will emerge showing which battles typically yield gains and which battles yield losses.
- **Put a temporary pin in it.** Sometimes the wisest move is to step back and hit the pause button. Saying something like: "I appreciate that perspective. Let me think about what you've said and get back to you tomorrow" gives you space to assess whether you're in orange or banana territory.
- **Seek a different perspective.** When unsure about a potential battle, run it by someone with a different conflict style. Christine, my risk-averse best friend balances my impulsive tendencies, while I occasionally nudge her toward uncertainty. She's taught me that every ounce of energy spent fighting unnecessary battles is energy unavailable for the truly important ones.

The juice worth the squeeze framework has saved me countless hours of frustration and relationship damage. But more importantly, it's helped me focus my energy on the battles that genuinely matter—the ones that create real change for teams and organizations.

When you stop fighting every conceptual banana and start choosing your oranges wisely, you don't just become more effective. You become the kind of delivery change agent people *want* to work with—someone who brings solutions, not just problems, and who creates positive change without destroying relationships in the process.

Connect the Dots and Take Action

Throughout this chapter, we've journeyed inward to explore the most critical factor in your effectiveness as a delivery change agent: you. We've examined the internal patterns that can either accelerate or sabotage your impact:

- **The feedback conundrum.** How our fear of criticism blocks the very growth we need most, and why we can't give what we can't receive.
- **Hidden motives**. The uncomfortable truth about when our "help" serves our ego more than our team, and how to recognize when fear drives our actions.
- **Curiosity versus judgment.** The power of approaching situations with genuine wonder rather than predetermined assumptions, and practical tools to reclaim childlike curiosity.
- **Emotional intelligence**. Managing our reactions so they enhance rather than hijack our effectiveness, from creating an emotional dashboard to developing your personal pause button.
- **Strategic battles.** Learning when the juice is worth the squeeze—how to choose your fights wisely and focus energy on changes that matter.

These aren't just "nice to have" soft skills. They're the invisible foundation that makes *everything else in this book possible*. You can learn every framework, know every technique, and understand every process—but if you can't manage your triggers, maintain your presence, or regulate your emotional responses, your technical expertise becomes irrelevant.

The most effective people I've worked with aren't necessarily the most technically gifted. They're the ones who've done the hard internal work—who can stay curious when they want to judge, remain composed when they feel attacked, and choose understanding over being right. They've learned that their greatest tool isn't their knowledge of scrum or agility, it's their ability to show up as the person their teams, partners, and leaders need them to be.

Here's my challenge for you:

Personal growth is a practice, not a project. Here's your starting point:

Weeks 1 and 2	Weeks 3 and 4	Month 2	Month 3 and beyond
Build Awareness	Establish Your Foundation	Deepen Your Practice	Integrate and Mentor
Complete the questions-to-statements ratio exercise from the Curious Person's Advantage section --- Consider the situations that generally cause you to react. Identify those emotional triggers --- Practice creating your emotional dashboard—asking "What am I feeling right now? Where do I feel it in my body? What triggered it?" --- Notice when you're trying to win versus trying to understand	Develop your personal pause button phrases like "That's interesting, can you provide additional context?" --- Begin asking yourself reflective questions that cause you to pause: "What can I learn here?" and "How do I want to show up?" --- Practice saying "I might be wrong" in low stakes situations --- Make your emotional dashboard part of your daily routine	Seek feedback from trusted colleagues about your patterns and blind spots --- Keep a journal of situations where you chose curiosity over judgment --- Experiment with the "love or fear" motive check before giving feedback --- Practice the "juice worth the squeeze" framework on smaller battles	Continue tracking your growth in areas where you've identified improvement opportunities --- Mentor others in the practices that have served you best --- Apply the TMMY rule—asking "Will this matter in 10 minutes? 10 months? 10 years?" before choosing battles --- Continue running the "love or fear" test before offering feedback or pushing agendas

Remember, this work never ends. The goal isn't perfection—it's progress. Every time you choose presence over distraction, curiosity over judgment, or understanding over winning, you're not just becoming a better delivery change agent. You're becoming a better leader, colleague, and human being.

The teams you serve will feel the difference, even if they can't name it. Your stakeholders will trust you more deeply. Your influence will grow not through force, but through the magnetic power of your authentic leadership.

--

And here we are!

You've learned to spot organizational dysfunction, connect your work to what leaders care about, and manage yourself so you can create positive change without burning bridges.

You, my friend, are not the same delivery change agent who originally opened this book.

- You see patterns others miss.
- You understand what drives business outcomes.
- You know how to influence systems, not just teams.
- Most importantly, you show up as the kind of person others want to partner with.

The delivery change agents who become truly indispensable are the ones who solve systemic problems while building authentic relationships. You've got *all* the pieces now to do just that.

Now go! Go out and create the incredible impact you're capable of making.

Conclusion

Your Mic Drop Moment

You are not the same you who started reading this book. When you first picked this up, you sensed your potential for greater impact. You wanted to translate your expertise into visible results. You were ready to evolve into the leader your organization needs and wants.

And you did the work. You absorbed frameworks for spotting organizational dysfunction. You learned techniques for building relationships with leaders. You developed tools for managing yourself effectively. But here's what really changed: **You now see what others miss**.

When you connect team headaches to the organizational dysfunction causing them, *everything* shifts. Teams stop "being busy" and start solving complex challenges that create real impact. Leaders stop getting boring status updates and start receiving insights that guide critical strategic decisions. Organizations trade speed for focused intentionality—and get better results because of it.

You've accumulated a powerful set of tools designed to discover the spark of a dumpster fire before it ignites, transform your team's work into business impact that can't be ignored, address organizational dysfunction at the root, keep your cool so you can truly help others, and (most importantly) be a trusted partner.

And here's the beautiful part: *every* delivery change agent brings their own unique strengths to this work. This diversity is exactly why I've recommended multiple approaches throughout these chapters. Like a "choose your own adventure" series, *you* get to pick the techniques that align with your natural strengths and interests.

Do you naturally gravitate toward others? Take what you've learned and go build powerful connections with leaders. Do you lean toward data and research? Awesome—then identifying organizational patterns and making sense out of ambiguous data is your jam. Do you love connecting the dots and seeing the bigger picture? Use that systems thinking mind to identify the broader dysfunction causing those frustrating team problems. Do you live for facilitating thought-provoking conversations? Channel that enthusiasm into surfacing dysfunction and driving meaningful change. Do you thrive on self-awareness and emotional growth? Transform those judgmental impulses into sincere curiosity instead.

The goal isn't to become the delivery change agent GOAT (the Greatest of All Time—we're not giving out trophies here). Just leverage what you're already pretty damn good at and build from there. Figure out what lights your inner fire and follow that natural spirit.

 *So, where do I begin?*

Start where you feel most confident and enthusiastic. Ask yourself: "What lights my soul? What makes my heart smile?" Honor whatever rises because that is your ideal jumping off point. Yours. No one else's.

Maybe you'll begin by leveraging the People Plan—new relationships invigorate you. You could meticulously track unplanned work since you love consolidating and analyzing data. Perhaps you'll trace team problems back to their organizational roots since you thrive on uncovering systemic dysfunction. You may even guide an RCA workshop—you live for those authentic discovery conversations. Or maybe you'll capture a week's worth of emotional triggers because you can't lead others until you can truly regulate yourself.

You're already on this journey. And the professionals who create the strongest impact do exactly what you're doing now. They deliberately *look up* while still supporting their teams. They connect their daily work to what leaders care about. They build legit relationships instead of just surface-level networking bullshit. And they know this: it gets smoother the more you practice it.

You're ready for this. You have everything you need to claim your place as the go-to person for solving what matters most. Now, go—and make it happen for yourself.

I'm so totally rooting for you.

Appendix

Stop Thinking, Start Doing

Reading about these tools won't change anything. But using them will. Within this appendix are clean, simple templates for the key frameworks that will help you build relationships, identify the root of the problems, and spot the waste that's bleeding your organization dry. Pick one and start today.

Your People Plan

Your "People Plan" will come in handy when good ideas go nowhere because you don't have the right relationships to make change happen. This plan helps you stop hoping that people will listen and start building the connections to get things done. Perfect for when you need leadership buy-in, want to expand your influence beyond your team, or when you're ready to turn your expertise into real organizational impact.

Your People Plan	
About Them	
Who is your stakeholder?	**What gets them out of bed?**
About You	
What's *your* why?	**What do you want to achieve?**
Your Plan	
How will you connect?	**What action will you take next?**

The Problem Identification Worksheet

When you're facing a team or organizational challenge and want to avoid jumping straight to solutions, lean on the problem identification worksheet. This tool forces you to slow down, understand what's really happening, and test your assumptions before taking action. Perfect for when teams are struggling, stakeholders are frustrated, or when previous "fixes" haven't worked. Use it solo, with your partners, or with your team to ensure that you're solving the right problem, not just the obvious (or easiest) one.

The Problem Identification Worksheet	
Question	**Example**
What do you want to fix?	
What's going wrong right now?	
What's your guess about how to fix it?	
How will you test your guess?	
How will you know if it worked?	
What might get in the way?	

Skills and Strengths Assessment

You're tired of having single points of failure on your team or watching work pile up because only one person knows how to do those critical tasks. This assessment shows you exactly where knowledge silos exist and what cross-training opportunities are missing. Perfect when someone can't take vacation, work gets stuck waiting for "the expert," or when you need to make the case for building T-shaped team members who can handle multiple types of work.

	Skills and Strengths Assessment							

Skill Experience Key:

- Green: Proficient
- Yellow: Learning
- Red: Needs Training
- Blank: Beginner

Downtime Waste Identification Chart

You know something's wrong with how work flows through your organization, but you can't quite put your finger on exactly what's bleeding time and money. This chart helps you systematically hunt down the hidden waste that's making everyone crazy and slowing delivery to a crawl. Fill out this chart when teams are constantly busy but nothing seems to get done, when you need concrete examples to show leadership what's broken, or when you're ready to stop complaining about problems and start fixing them.

Downtime Waste Identification Chart

Defects:	Work that has to be redone or fixed
Overproduction:	Building features nobody asked for or needs
Waiting:	Delays for approvals, decisions, or other people
Non-Utilized Talent:	Wasting people's skills and knowledge
Transportation:	Moving information unnecessarily between systems
Inventory:	Work piling up without delivering value
Motion:	Repetitive manual tasks that could be automated
Extra Processing:	Overcomplicating simple problems

Waste	What I observed	Root Cause	Potential Solution	Who to involve

Root Cause Analysis (RCA) Template

Something went awry and you need to figure out what exactly caused it, instead of just slapping a band-aid on the symptom (because honestly, you're running out of band-aids). This template helps you dig under "human error" or "process failure" to find the **real** root cause. Use when problems keep recurring, when you need to solve problems systematically, or when you want to prevent the same issue from blindsiding your team again (and again, and again).

Root Cause Analysis (RCA) Template	
Date of RCA/ Participants	
What happened?	
When did this happen?/What's the frequency?	
What was the impact?	
Why did it happen? *(5 Why's)*	
What evidence supports this?	
What is the solution?	
How will we know the solution worked?	
Next steps? (Include owner & date due)	

Index

www.ingramcontent.com/pod-product-compliance
Lightning Source LLC
LaVergne TN
LVHW050632100826
845148LV00011B/1840

* 9 7 8 1 6 0 6 4 9 5 6 6 7 *